THE
ESSENTIAL
GNOSTIC
GOSPELS

Alan Jacobs is a retired art dealer and has been interested
in comparative religion and mysticism from an early age.
For a number of years he has been Chairman of the Ramana
Maharshi Foundation UK.

As a poet he is published regularly in the magazine *Reflections*.

THE ESSENTIAL
GNOSTIC GOSPELS

Including

The Gospel of Thomas

The Gospel of Mary Magdalene

Alan Jacobs

WATKINS PUBLISHING

LONDON

Distributed in the USA and Canada by Sterling Publishing Co., Inc.
387 Park Avenue South, New York, NY 10016

This edition first published in the UK and USA 2006 by
Watkins Publishing, Sixth Floor, Castle House,
75–76 Wells Street, London W1T 3QH

1 3 5 7 9 10 8 6 4 2

Designed and typeset by Jerry Goldie

Printed and bound in Great Britain

Library of Congress Cataloging-in-Publication Data Available

ISBN-10: 1-84293-203-9
ISBN-13: 978-1-84293-203-2

For information about custom editions, special sales, premium and
corporate purchases, please contact Sterling Special Sales
Department at 800-805-5489 or specialsales@sterlingpub.com.

Contents

FOREWORD

As discovered at Nag Hammadi, the Gnostic Gospels were mainly written in Early Coptic and Classical Greek. They formed a private collection of Gnostic scriptures buried in the Egyptian desert. Of the codicils, a few were already known and many others were new. They were severely fragmented, and full of lacunas.

As a brief introduction to each poem, I have given a short synopsis of its history, authorship and content. To provide a clear, readable text that preserves the essential meaning, with as much clarity and simplicity as possible, has been my principal aim. Obscurities and needless repetitions have been excluded in some tracts.

The texts selected, from the 53 that were discovered, are chosen because they are, potentially, of greater interest to the contemporary reader than others which abound in archaisms and strangely coined proper names whose derivation and usage has largely been lost.

The Gospels chosen throw light on the intimate relationship of Jesus and his disciples, and reveal many sayings of Christ which are not found in the New Testament. For example, in The Gospel of Mary Magdalene and The Hidden Book of James, we find some hitherto unknown details of Christ's relationship with these favoured disciples. Other texts explain the structure of Gnostic cosmology.

I am most grateful to the Very Reverend Dr Vrej N Nersessian for his scholarly introduction, explaining the history and significance of the Gospels, and his overview of the text. I must also express my thanks to the staff of the British Library who helped me to find all the known literature and translations of these tracts, and Annie Bridges and Shelagh Boyd for their editorial assistance.

Alan Jacobs

INTRODUCTION

Jewish beliefs marked Christianity permanently until the fourth century, when Jewish Christians who had been prominent in the New Testament were reduced to a remnant. Those who survived had their own *Gospel according to the Hebrews*.

Christian teaching had become hostile to Judaism, as evidenced in the *Letter of Barnabas*, written in the second century. It was claimed that an evil spirit had inspired the Jews to misunderstand the purposes of God throughout their history. Ignatius, in the second century, did not hesitate to talk about Jesus as "our God", whatever might be the objections of Jews. In his *Letter to the Magnesians* he wrote, "God is one and has revealed himself to his Son Jesus Christ, who is his Word issuing from silence." But he said that the zeal of the Christians in Ephesus had been aroused by "God's blood" and begged the Christians in Rome not to try to prevent his own martyrdom: "Let me imitate the suffering of my God." He was not interested in offering any philosophical defence of such expressions, for the main thrust of his message was a plea for Christians to unite; he was less interested in finding common ground with Jews or with any others who did not share his faith. His life's ambition was "to become God's wheat, and I am ground by the teeth of wild beasts so that I may become Christ's pure loaf ... Come fire, cross, a battle with wild beasts, the wrenching of bones, the mangling of limbs, the crushing of my whole body, the cruel tortures of the Devil – only let me get to Jesus Christ." He also said, "my Love is crucified", meaning that his own human passions had died with Jesus.

Paul had expressed a similar sentiment, but Ignatius went beyond the more balanced Paul by saying plainly that he was "in love with death". The Armenian poet Gregory of Narek (951–1003) likens his relationship to Christ to "the wick in the candle":

You crave oil, and in this oil you placed a wick

which exemplifies your union, without imperfection,

with our condition, formed and woven with your love of

mankind.

[Gregory of Narek, *Book of Lamentations*, Erevan, 1985]

Christianity's main partners in the fourth century were not Jews but pagans, or, more often, people who were seeking reality in religion and not finding it in either Judaism or paganism. The great question was, What did such seekers have to believe in order to be Christians? If Christianity was no longer a Jewish sect, how far could it go as it left its Palestinian birthplace? Could it go on to speak about mysteries hitherto left to what Ignatius had called "the silence"?

The acceptance by the Church in 381 of the full divinity of Christ almost inevitably led to disputes about the relationship between divine and human natures. This issue had a resonance in the late Roman Empire beyond the interests of theologians because the Christian Gnostic movement was particularly strong in Egypt. Basilides, whom some scholars consider the most subtle of Gnostic thinkers (117–160) challenged the Orthodox Church on its teaching regarding the relationship of the divine and human natures in Christ. He had followers in fourth-century Egypt, where many schools of Gnosticism had flourished attracting wide support, and Greek Gnostic writings were being translated into Coptic. They wrote treatises to expound their teaching, which they attributed to well-known biblical figures like Seth, Isaiah and the Apostles, or to oral traditions received from Christ himself.

Although Gnostics and the early Church fathers were in some measure addressing the same problem – how to understand the cosmic significance of the life and teaching of Jesus – their approaches to it were fundamentally different. For although the various Gnostic schools differed a good deal between themselves about matters of detail, they all agreed that the material world had come into being as the result of a cosmic accident and that the demiurge who had fashioned it was not the true God. They also agreed that the spirits of men and women had become trapped in material bodies but belonged by nature to the spiritual world, which was perfect, and they used the vivid metaphor "gold in mud" to describe the human condition.

Christ was a totally spiritual being, an aeon or emanation of the supreme God, who had sent him into the world to make men aware of their true spiritual state. In order to be understood by them, Christ entered into the man Jesus of Nazareth. Those who were willing to receive the knowledge (gnosis), that Christ imparted, obtained salvation. When they died their enlightened spirits could return to the realm of the supreme God where they belonged. The Gnostics were not interested in the human body because it was a part of the imperfect material world. It is this view of life which the doctrine of the pre-existence of the soul is intended to secure:

> Why have you snatched me away from my home,
>
> and brought me into this prison,
>
> and incarcerated me in this stinking body?
>
> …
>
> How far are the frontiers of this world of darkness?
>
> The way we have to go is far and never-ending
>
> [Mandaean text from the Ginza]

Such lamentations are constantly repeated in Gnostic literature. In the *Song of the Naasenes* the human self – here actually called the soul – is depicted as a stag in flight, seeking in vain the way of freedom from earthly fate:

> Now she wears the crown and beholds the light,
>
> now she is cast down into the depths of misery;

now she weeps, now she recovers her joy;

now she weeps and laughs at the same time;

now she is judged and passes away in death;

now she is born anew

and without hope of escape, the hapless,

wandering soul is shut up in a labyrinth of woe.

[Hippolyt, V,1]

Pistis Sophia, a Coptic Gnostic text of the late third century (British Library Ms. Add.5114), is a work of this kind, which begins:

> It came to pass that when Jesus had risen from the dead, that
> he passed eleven years discoursing with his disciples, and
> instructing them only up to the regions of the First
> Commandments and up to the regions of the First Mystery,
> that within the Veil, within the First Commandment, which
> is the four-and-twentieth mystery without and below – those
> four-and-twenty which are in the second space of the First
> Mystery which is before all mysteries – the Father in the
> form of a dove.

Upholders of the Catholic tradition could not project themselves as being completely dismissive of the material world, which they believed had been created by God, even though it was flawed by evil. Christ, God's Son, in their view became a man, not just as a way of communicating with mankind, but as a means of restoring the whole creation to a rightful relationship with God. His humanity was therefore integral to his mission: he lived a fully human life, he died as all men do, and he rose bodily from the dead as the first-born of the new creation.

Given this centuries-long debate between Gnostics and the early Church about the importance of Christ's humanity, it was inevitable that strong feelings should have been aroused in Egypt by the theological dispute about the relationship between the divine and human natures of Christ. The "Adoptionist" theory and the objection to calling the Blessed Virgin Mary "Theotokos" (literally "the God-bearer") were both attempts by Gnostics to promote the thought of Christ being entirely spiritual and not reduce Christ to such dependence on a human mother.

The immediate effect of the thinking within the Church was to make many members defensive about anything intellectual. If the heretics appealed to philosophy, then philosophy must be vain, deceit, human speculation rather than revealed truth. The influence of the negative attitude persisted for a long period. The opposition to Gnosticism leads to an extremely literalistic doctrine of the resurrection of the flesh, but also of a strictly earthly hope for a millennial reign of Christians at Jerusalem.

Looking back with the advantage of detachment of hindsight, while early research regarded the Gnostic movements as purely Christian, a perversion of the Christian faith into a speculative theology, modern research has, however, made it abundantly clear that it was really a religious movement of pre-Christian origin. In all its forms, its mythology and theology arise from a definite attitude to life and an interpretation of human existence derived therefrom. In general, we may call it a redemptive religion based on dualism. This is what gives it an affinity to Christianity, an affinity of which even its adherents were aware.

Consequently, Gnosticism and Christianity have affected each other in a number of different directions from the earliest days of the Christian movement. Although certain features in the Gnostic imagery claimed a rightful place within the Church, other Gnostic ideas were not only ignored, but bitterly resisted.

At the time when Gnostic movements were shaping their mythologies there was no fixed canon of the New Testament writings, and Gnostic teachers were proud to be able to produce *Secret Sayings of Jesus*, accounts of what Jesus had said to his disciples between the Resurrection and the

Ascension. The Gospels, Acts, Letters and Apocalypses widely current were not limited to those which in the course of time became the New Testament. There were also Gnostic texts which "the Church" did not recognise as authoritative and which were excluded from the canon.

In 1945, in a village in Upper Egypt called Nag Hammadi, a camel driver uncovered a jar containing the remains of thirteen codices. Analysis of the materials used in the bindings of the codices shows that they had been produced in the area in which they were found. Dates on letters and grain receipts indicate a date in the middle of the fourth century AD. References to the Coptic monk Pachom were proof that the volumes had been in the possession of the Pachomian monks who inhabited the area.

The works in the collection may have been a library in use by Gnostics, or they may have been copied by monks in Upper Egypt who were intending to refute Gnostic claims. Or, because orthodoxy and heresy were so intermingled among ascetics in that region, they may have served to defend the practices of the monks, while the more heretical works were later separated and entombed, when, in 367, Athanasius sent out a letter condemning apocryphal books.

Gnosticism was Egyptian Christianity, gradually supressed by Orthodox Christianity, with claims that Christian Gnostic writings were heretical. Its books were burned except those hidden by the monks.

The writings in the collection were translated into Coptic from Greek. A few that provided striking examples of the teaching of the Gnostics were published within a decade and became well known: *The Gospel of Truth, The Treatise on Resurrection, The Gospel of Thomas, The Gospel of Philip, The Apocryphon of John, The Wisdom of Jesus.* These writings represent an ascetic position with regard to the material world and its passions. One of the most striking features of the teaching is the elaborate mythology that explains how this world of darkness, dominated by a demonic god and his powers, came into being. Most of these myths begin with a harmonious unfolding of the heavenly world from an indescribable divinity. The divinity may be represented as a "one" beyond all beings or may be given the epithet

"Mother–Father". Since matter, passions, darkness and discord have nothing in common with the divine, the myths eventually tell the story of a "fall" or a "flaw" in the heavenly realm. Often, this "flaw" is the restless desire of the youngest of the divine beings, Wisdom (*Pistis Sophia*, British Library, Add. 5114). She may be seeking the divine Father above or she may try to give birth without her heavenly consort, as the Mother–Father does.

Alan Jacobs, a poet relying on his personal and practical knowledge of the mystical path in religion, has selected extracts from 53 Gnostic texts that shed light on these esoteric doctrines. His inspired poetic translations give us a glimpse of the more attractive side of Gnosticism. Whatever else Jesus Christ might have been, the Church refused to make him a demigod, and the various forms of speculation that were defined as Gnostic coined terms and conceptions which did attempt to bridge the gulf. The most popular Gospel is that of Thomas, sometimes called the "fifth Gospel" for its very close resemblance to the canonical Gospels. It contains 114 "sayings" of Jesus [*logia*], introduced by the simple formula "Jesus said", including the parable of the sower, the grain of mustard seed, the tares, the pearl of great price, the leaven, the lost sheep, the treasure hidden in a field. But the Coptic text almost never corresponds word for word with that of the canonical Gospels. The centre of interest is gnosis, a profound knowledge that depends on the interpretation of the secret words (*logion* 1), and begins with knowledge of oneself (*logion* 3). The person of the Revealer is himself a mystery. To know him will make Thomas the equal of Jesus (*logion* 13). It is this gnosis that Jesus brings, "that which the eye has not seen, and the ear has not heard" (*logion* 17). The disciples already possess the beginning of the truth (*logion* 18), but they will have to "work" in order that gnosis may produce its fruits in them (*logion* 20). They will be watchful with regard to the evil powers, those "robbers" who threaten them (*logion* 21). Let there be among them "a man forewarned", that is to say, a Gnostic sage.

It is significant that Gnosticism tends to produce an individualistic type of mysticism, in which the redemption, the ascent of the Self, is anticipated in meditation and ecstasy. Gnosis, which in its initial stages stood for the knowledge of man's predicament, ends with the vision of God. The purpose of all spiritual endeavour is to achieve the experience of the true Self, and that can be defined only in negative terms. There is this hymn of thanksgiving, which provides a good illustration of Gnostic spirituality :

> I became whole in thy truth
>
> and holy in thy righteousness
>
> All mine adversaries yielded before my face;
>
> I became the Lord's in the name of the Lord.
>
> I was justified by his loving kindness,
>
> and his peace endureth for ever and ever.
>
> Amen

[Odes of Solomon]

Gnostic authors speak of God in imagery that is both male and female. "I am the Father; I am the Mother; I am the Son," God says in *The Apocryphon of John*. Elsewhere a spirit of wisdom announces, "I am the Voice ... in the likeness of a female ... in the thought of the likeness of my masculinity ... I am androgynous ..." The unification of the sexes served in early Christianity as a symbol of salvation, and in the memorable announcement of St Paul in his Letter to the Galatians, in Christ "there is neither male nor female; for you are all one in Christ" (Gal. 3:28). Paul borrows this text from Gnostic literature. The theme of "making the male and female into a single one" is also explicit in *The Gospel of Thomas*. And in *The Gospel of Mary Magdalene* the apostle Levi admonishes Peter "for doubting a woman as worthy", reminding Peter that:

> If Jesus made her upright,
>
> who are we to disown her?
>
> Jesus knew her well, that's

why he loved her more than us.

Let's be penitent ...

In the famous Gnostic text called *The Pistis Sophia*, the most provocative aspect is that the extended discipleship of Jesus is revealed as including both males and females. In fact, women play a uniquely prominent role in this story and dialogue with Jesus that provides insights and answers to the stucture of the universe and the mission of the trinitarian Godhead through the descent and ascent of Pistis Sophia. The declaratory statements of the female disciples in this text are three times more expansive than those of the male apostles. It gives special meaning to the words of the prophet Joel (Ch.2:28–29) telling us that at the end of days, the spirit will be poured out upon both sons and daughters. It is this greater transmutation that will take place as we go from human intelligence to higher intelligence, from rational mind into super mind, balanced by love.

Also shared by Gnosticism and Orthodox writers was a sense that Christ was really polymorphous, that he had many different appearances depending on who was perceiving him. The chameleon-like changeability of Christ in early Christian art may be linked to the belief that God "hath no form nor comeliness"(Isaiah 53: 2).

Christianity, having opted for the most "visual", "tangible" and "materialist" expressions, has deprived its followers of the need to "seek", to "search", "to look for the 'hidden". The formulaic definition of the "mystery profound" within fixed doctrines has meant that these positions outside their historical context have become incomprehensible, irrelevant and absurd. Today, Christianity is in constant need of reinventing itself.

The twelfth-century Armenian poet Nerses Shnorhali (1102–73) teaches that man, in spite of his fallen state, is still in "the image of God, and paradise is his habitation". Claiming a secret divine wisdom specially revealed to the initiates – "to be the Revealer of the hidden treasures" – humans ascend to the spiritual and to the rational enjoyment of the good tidings of God, which the eye has not seen, the ear has not heard, which the heart of man has not recalled, and which God has prepared for his loved ones. For the modern reader, Alan Jacobs' inspired poetic translation has captured the awesome beauty of the original Gospels, "to make us finders of the hidden treasures":

> His disciples asked,
> "On which day will you
> make yourself known to us?"
> Lord Jesus replied,
> "When you rid yourselves
> of guilt and shame."

Alan Jacobs' skill in his craft has freed Gnostic texts of their tedious and grotesque theosophical speculations to reveal a completely different aspect – mystical, devotional, poetical.

Revd Dr Vrej N. Nersessian
Curator, The British Library
Christian Middle East Section

THE ESSENTIAL
GNOSTIC
GOSPELS

THE FABLE OF
THE PEARL

A dramatic Greek myth depicting the Soul's bodily incarnation and its eventual liberation. Attributed to Jude Thomas the Apostle, it summarises the "Gnostic Call" to awaken from the dream of life into Self or God Realisation.

FROM THE APOCRYPHAL ACTS OF
THE APOSTLE THOMAS

When I was an innocent child I lived in my father's house,
enjoying the love of all who reared me.
Then my parents sent me from our Eastern home,
with enough goods for a long trip.

They burdened me with treasure light enough to bear alone:
gold from ancient hills, silver plate and goblets,
emeralds from India and agates from Kosa,
but they stripped me of my robe of glory.
This they'd woven from generous love,
with a jewel-studded purple cloak that fitted well.

They drew up a deed, impressing it on my heart and memory.
"Go down to Egypt, fetch that one pearl
from the ocean bed, kept by a fierce serpent.
Then you can wear your robe again, your precious cloak,
and with your brother inherit our kingdom."

I left with two friends,
for the path was dangerous and I was young.
I passed through Maishan, and their greedy merchants,
then came to Babel, and entered seedy Sarburg.
I'd arrived in Egypt.

My friends left. I went close to the serpent;
I stayed at an inn until he fell asleep
and I could seize the pearl.

Since I was One and stayed with my Self
I was unrecognised by my fellow guests.
But I saw one youth like myself,
a son of the King, an initiated one.

He introduced himself and became my friend,
someone in whom I could confide.
He warned me about the Egyptians,
and making friends with the impure.

But I had to wear clothes like theirs

or they might suspect I was a stranger
who planned to steal the pearl.
Yet they suspected I wasn't one of them,
and slyly bedevilled me,
giving me strong drink and spiced meats.

I soon forgot I was the King's son
and slaved for their Pharoah.
I even forgot the pearl.
After their heavy food and rich drink
I fell into a deep sleep.

My parents heard about all that happened and were very sad.
It was announced in our kingdom that all must return.
The Kings of Parthia and Eastern nobles
decided I mustn't stay in Egypt.

They sent me a letter,
"From your father the King of Kings. Your mother,
the Eastern Queen, your brother, next in line, all send greetings.
Awake from sleep! Remember you're the son of a Great King,
see to whom you're enslaved!

Recall the precious pearl and why you left for Egypt,
and your robe of glory and your purple cloak, so you can
wear them again and your name be written in the Hero's Book,
and with your brother succeed to our kingdom."

This letter from the King was sealed by his right hand
and contained a message warning against the evil folk
of Babel and Sarburg.

It flew before me carried by an eagle, king of the birds.
It landed beside me and the bird began to sing!
The golden tone of his song woke me up!
I held and stroked him, broke the seal, and read.

Then I remembered I was the son of a Great King
and that my pure soul yearned and craved for its own likeness.
I recalled the priceless pearl for which I had gone down
into the land of Egypt.

I went to the serpent and charmed him to sleep,
constantly repeating, again and again, my father's name,
and that of my brother, next in line,
and my mother, Queen of the East.

I seized the precious pearl and fled quickly,
to return to my beloved father.
I threw off my filthy Egyptian smock, leaving it behind.
Recollecting my Self I went east to come home.

This clarion letter lit my path, and by its clarity encouraged me,
and by its love, led me on.
I remembered my robe and purple cloak,

which I had left in my parents' house,
and the treasures they'd given me.

When I pictured the robe in its full glory
it suddenly seemed to be a reflection of my Real Self.
I saw my own Self in this clear mirror, knowing the see-er
and the seen were not two but One.
The King of Kings was imaged there
shimmering all over, as the true Gnosis.

I saw He was poised to sing,
and I heard the murmur of His song.
"I Am That Power, which acted in the acts of he
who was reared in his father's house."

I noted my strength grew according to my efforts.
With kingly grace He poured love on me,
with heraldic hands hastening me to drink.

My love raced to greet Him, I expanded,
cladding myself with His rainbow hues.
I threw His royal cloak over my whole Self.

Well robed I entered the pearly gate
of prostration and adoration.
I bowed my head, kneeled and worshipped
in my Father's Presence.

His will I obeyed,
in response to the fulfilment of His promise.

He received me with open arms and holy joy.
I was with Him in His kingdom.
The seraphim praised Him with loud song.

"Hallelujah! Holy, holy, holy is the Lord of Hosts,
the whole Earth is full of His glory."

He had honoured His covenant,
that I would come to His Court,
The King of Kings.

For I had found the pearl beyond price
and would be with Him Eternally.

THE GOSPEL
OF THOMAS

A primary scripture of the Early Eastern Church, recorded by Jude Thomas the Apostle, relating intimate Gnostic sayings of Jesus to his disciples, many of which do not appear in the New Testament. Originally written in Greek before AD 200.

These are the secret words of Almighty God,
which Lord Jesus Christ uttered
and were scribed by his disciple Thomas.

He said, "He who comprehends the inner meaning
of these words will be immortal.

Permit whoever seeks never to cease
from seeking until he finds.

When he succeeds he will be turned around;
when he's so turned he'll be amazed
and shall rule over the All.

If those who lead you say 'God's Kingdom's in Heaven,'
then birds will fly there first.
If they say 'It's in the sea,'
the fish will swim there first.

For God's Kingdom dwells in your heart and all around you;
when you know your Self you too shall be known!

You'll be aware that you're the sons and daughters
of our living Father.
But if you fail to know your own Self
you're in hardship and are that hardship."

His disciples enquired,
"Should we fast? How should we pray?
Should we give to charity? What should we eat?"

Lord Jesus replied,
"Don't lie! Don't do what you hate! All's seen by Heaven.
There's nothing hidden that won't be made known.
There's nothing secret that will stay concealed
without first being shown.

Happy is the lion that a man will eat;
the lion will become a man.
Cursed is the man whom the lion eats
for that lion will become a man.

Man is like a skilled angler who casts his net
and draws it up, full of fish.
Among them he finds big and small fish.
He throws back the small and keeps the large.

He who has his ears wide open, let him hear!

A sower went to sow.
He filled his hand with seeds
and scattered them on the field.

Some fell on the path,
rooks flew down and ate them;
some fell on rocks and failed to root.

Others fell on thorns that choked them,
and worms ate them up.
Some fell on good soil and grew good fruit,
sixty times the measure and even double.

I've set fire to this world, to keep it blazing
until it burns away.
Heaven will pass away;
that which is above heaven will also pass away.

Dead souls don't live, live souls don't die;
yet when you treat dead souls you bring them alive.

When you're in the Light what will you do?
At birth you were One, then you made two.
What will you do?"

The disciples asked, "We know you'll leave us.
Who'll then rule over us?"

Jesus replied,
"Wherever you arrive, go to James who is righteous,
because of whom, even heaven and earth came into existence;
now tell me whom I resemble."

Simon Peter answered him first,
"You're like a righteous angel."
Matthew said, "You're like a sage or lover of wisdom."
Thomas said, "My lips won't let me say you're like anyone."

Jesus replied, "I'm no longer your Master
because you've drunk from living water.
You're enlivened by the bubbling source
which I've caused to flow."

He took Thomas on one side and addressed
three sayings of Almighty God to him.
When Thomas returned they enquired,
"What did Jesus say?"

Thomas replied, "If I tell you what he said
you'll pick up stones and hurl them at me;
fire will rise up from them and burn you all up!"

Lord Jesus then said, "If you fast you'll get into sin;
if you pray for boons you'll be condemned;
when you give alms you may wound your spirit.

When you go to other lands, into their countryside,
if they welcome you, eat what they provide and heal their sick.
What enters your sight won't harm you,
but what comes out of your mouth can defile you.

When you see He who's unborn from a womb,
prostrate and worship, for He's your Father.

Men believe I've come to bring peace to this world,
but they don't understand that I've come to bring
divisions on earth, fire, struggle and strife.

If there are five in a house, three will fight two,
two will fight three.
Father versus son, son against father;
they'll stand up better being alone.

I'll show you what no eye has seen, no ear has heard,
no hand has touched, and what is not yet risen in men's hearts."

The disciples then said, "Tell us what our end will be."

He answered, "Have you seen the beginning
that you may know the end?
Where there's a beginning there's no end.
Happy is the man or woman who can stand
bravely at the beginning.
He or she shall know the end and won't taste death."

The disciples then enquired about the Kingdom of Heaven.

Jesus replied, "It's like a grain of mustard,
smaller than other seeds, but when it falls on ploughed ground
it grows a large stem and shelters the birds."

Mary asked Lord Jesus, "Whom are your disciples like?"
He replied, "Like small children
living in a field which isn't theirs.
When the owners return they'll demand their land back;
the disciples have to strip off their outer pretensions
and pay back their loan.

So if the landlord of the house knows a burglar is coming
he'll stay awake before he breaks in.
He'll not allow the rogue to steal his goods.

So, watch this world; get ready for deeds with great strength,

otherwise thieves will find a way to break into you,
and the reward you expect, they'll get.

In your heart let there be a man of understanding!
When the corn ripens he comes in haste,
sickle in hand, and reaps!
He who has his ears wide open, let him hear!"

Lord Jesus saw babies being breastfed.
He said to his disciples, "These infants being suckled
are like those who enter my Father's House."

They answered, "Shall we, being as children,
come into His Kingdom?"

Jesus replied, "Make the two into One
and the inner as the outer and the outer as the inner,
the above as below, the male and female into a single One.

So the male isn't male and the female isn't female any more.
When you make two eyes into a single eye,
a hand into a hand, a foot into a foot,
a picture into a picture, then you'll enter the Kingdom.

I'll choose you, as one from a thousand;
you'll stand bravely, being a single One."

His disciples said, "Show us that place where you are;
we need to search for it."

He answered, "If you have ears then pay attention and listen!

There's perfect Light at the heart of a Man of Light;
he lights up the whole world. If he fails to shine there's
darkness.

If you don't give up the world you won't find the Kingdom.
If you don't keep the Sabbath as a real Sabbath,
you won't know my Father.

I stood bravely in the middle of the world; I came in a body.
I found them drunk! None were thirsty.

My soul was afflicted for mankind,
for they are blind at heart and do not see.
Empty, they enter this world, empty they'll leave!

But now they're drunk!
When they sober up they'll change their Knowledge.

A fortified city built on a high mountain will not fall,
nor is it a secret.

What you hear clearly between your two ears,
shout from the rooftops.
Nobody lights a lamp and hides it;
instead they put it on a stand
so everyone can enjoy its light.

If a blind man guides the blind,
they'll both slip into a ditch.
It's impossible to enter the house of a strong man
and win it by force.
One must bind his hands, then one can enter.
Have no cares from dawn until night for what you try."

His disciples asked,
"On which day will you make yourself known to us?"

Lord Jesus replied, "When you rid yourselves
of guilt and shame and tear off your old rags
and trample them beneath your feet like children.

Then you'll see the Son of He who is the living God,
and you'll never need fear again.

Many years you've yearned to hear
these words of God which I give you.
You've no one else from whom to hear them;
there'll be days when you look for me and fail to find me.

To he who holds the Truth in his hand,
more shall be handed; he who doesn't hold the Truth,
even the little he has shall be taken away.
Be your Self, especially when you're approaching death."

His disciples enquired,
"Who are you that you can say these words to us?"
Lord Jesus answered,
"From what I say can't you see who I am?
But you're like those Jews who love the tree and shun its fruit,
or love the fruit and shun the tree.

He who blasphemes against my father shall be forgiven,
but he who blasphemes against the holy Spirit
shall not be forgiven, in earth or in heaven.

Grapes aren't picked from thorn bushes,
nor are figs found on thistles.

A good man brings virtue out of his barn;
a bad man brings ill will from the evil stored in his heart.
He spreads guile from his heart's plenty
and spreads wickedness.

From Adam until John the Baptist,
among children of the womb
there's none higher than he.

John has a vision that won't be blurred.
But as I've said, he among you who becomes like a small child
shall know the kingdom and be greater than John.

If two make peace in their one house, they'll say with faith
to the mountain 'Move!' and it will move.

Happy are the solitary and those chosen,
for they shall find God's Kingdom.
If you seek it in your heart you shall enter again."

His disciples asked,
"On which day will peace for the dead come about?
When will a new world come?"

Jesus replied, "What you desire has already come,
but you don't realise it."

His disciples said, "Two dozen prophets spoke to Israel;
they all prophesied your true nature."

Jesus replied, "You've ignored he who lives with you,
and you've spoken about the dead.

He who knows this world has found a corpse;
he who has found a corpse, this world finds unworthy.

The Kingdom of heaven is like a farmer
who bought good seed;
his foe came one night, stole his seeds
and then sowed weeds.

The farmer forbade his workmen to hoe the weeds,
saying, 'In pulling the weeds you may ruin the wheat too.'

But I say, at harvest time the weeds will crop;
they must all be hoed and burnt!"

Jesus and his disciples saw a Samaritan
travelling to Judea carrying a lamb.

Jesus said, "Why does he bear that lamb?"

They answered, "To kill and eat it.
While it's alive he can't eat it,
only when it's dead can he dine."

Jesus then said, "You yourselves,
find the place of peace within,
or you too will be like dead lambs and be eaten!

I tell my cryptic parables to those worthy to hear them.
Whatever effort your right side may attempt,
don't let your left know what it tries.

There was a rich man who said, 'I'll use my wealth to sow,
reap and plant and fill up my barns so I lack nothing.'
That night he died.

He who has ears wide open, let him hear!

A man planned a feast; when he'd prepared the food
he sent his servant to invite the guests.
The servant met the first and said,
'My master asks you to dinner.'

The man answered, 'I've got money ready
for some merchants; they'll come this evening,
and I wish to place some orders, so I'm sorry, I can't come.'

He went to another and said,
'My master invites you to dinner.'
The man answered, 'I've just bought a farm.
I must collect the rents, so I'm sorry, I can't come.'

The servant went back and told his master
that those he'd invited couldn't come.

The master told his servant, 'Go out on the street
and bring any you can find so they may come and eat.'
So you see, busy business people
will not enter the house of my Father.

Show me the stone that the builders have rejected;
that one shall be my corner stone.

He who understands all but lacks Self Knowledge lacks all.

Be happy when you're reviled and harassed;
but peace won't be found if your mind harasses you at heart."

A man said to Jesus,
"Please tell my brothers to share my father's goods with me."

Jesus answered,
"Oh man, who made me to be a divider; is that who I am?

The harvest is great, the labourers are few and sluggish;
pray to the Lord to send good workmen.
There are many looking down the well,
but few are diving deeply.

I am the Light above them all; I am the All;
the All issues from me and reaches me.

Cut wood, I am there; lift stone, I am there.

Why did you come here to my countryside?
To see a reed shaken by the wind,
or a man clothed in soft garments?

Your kings and nobles wear fine robes
but do not know Truth!"

A woman from the mob that had gathered said,
"Blessed is the womb that gave birth to you, my Lord,
and the breasts that suckled you."

He answered, "Happy are all those who've heard my words,
the hidden secrets of my Father, The Living God,
and have kept them in good Faith.

For there may come a time when you'll say,
'Happy is the womb that didn't give birth,
and the breasts that didn't feed.'

He that loves the world, identifies with his body,
and he who does so, the world is unworthy of him.

He who's become rich, let him be king,
and he who has power, let him abandon it.

He who is near to me is close to the fire,
and he who is distant is far from my Kingdom.

Pictures are seen by men, but that pure Light
which reveals them lies veiled.

In the reflection of my Father's Light
His Light will be seen;
but His image will be hidden by His Light.

On the day you see the Light of your own true Self,
you'll rejoice!

But if you only see forms
which from the beginning were in you,
and don't die to them or know them,
how can you stand the Light?

Adam was created from a vast power and great fecundity.
He wasn't fit for you for had he been worthy
he wouldn't have known spiritual death.

Foxes have holes, birds boast nests;
the Son of Man has no den where he can
lay down his head and rest.

Decadent is the soul that depends on the body;
miserable is the man attached to the flesh.

Angels and Prophets will visit you
and hand you what is truly yours.
You must give back what's in your keeping.

Pray to your Self and ask,
'When will they come to collect what's theirs?'
Why do you clean only the lip of a cup when
He who made the inner also made the outer?

Follow me! My yoke is easy,
my lordship is gentle; you'll find peace."

The disciples asked,
"Who are you? So that we may trust you."

Lord Jesus replied,
"You merely contemplate the surface of heaven and earth,
but he who stands before you you don't know;
 nor do you know how to find out.

Search and you shall find! But what you've asked me
I held from telling you; now I wish to speak.
But you do not seek after Self Knowledge.

Don't waste good food on dogs; they leave it on a dung heap.
Don't hand pearls to pigs; they'll pollute them.

He who earnestly and persistently seeks, shall find!
To him who knocks hard, the door will be opened.

If you have money, don't lend just for interest,
but give it to him who needs it.

The Kingdom of Heaven is like a good woman
who takes leaven,
hides it in dough and bakes loaves.

Those that have ears to hear, let them hear!

The Kingdom of Heaven is also like a foolish woman
carrying a load of flour on a long road;
the sack splits and flour pours out, but she doesn't realise.
Because she doesn't see what has happened, she isn't worried,
but when she gets home her sack is empty.

The Kingdom of Heaven is like a brave soldier
wishing to slay a giant; he draws his sword at home
and strikes through the wall to test his confidence.
Then he goes and kills the giant."

His disciples said,
"Your mother and brothers are waiting outside."

He replied, "All those here who do the will of my Father
are my mother and brothers;
they're the ones who will enter
the Kingdom of Heaven."

The disciples showed Jesus a gold shekel, saying,
"Caesar's collectors demand taxes from us."
Jesus replied, "Hand to Caesar what is Caesar's,
to God what is God's, and what is mine hand to me.

He who doesn't reject his mother and father
because of my teaching
won't become my disciple,
for my mother gave me birth
but my real Mother gave me life.

Pity the Pharisees; they're like dogs
sleeping in an ox's shed.
They neither eat nor let the ox eat.

Blessed is the man who knows
when thieves will break into his house.
He can get up, collect himself,
and be ready to act before they come."

The disciples said, "Let's pray and fast today."
Jesus answered, "What sin have I committed
or by what have I been conquered?
When the bridegroom leaves the bridal chamber,
then we'll fast and pray.

He who knows his real Mother and Father,
can he be called the son of a whore?
When you make two into One you'll be sons of Man,
and if you command a mountain to move, it will move.

The Kingdom of Heaven is like the good shepherd
who owned a hundred sheep.
When the fattest was lost he left all the others until he found it.
He told his flock, 'I loved that one more than the rest.'

He who drinks my words with understanding
shall be like me,
and I shall become him
and the secret things will be revealed.

The Kingdom of Heaven is like the farmer
who owned a field with buried treasure
that he did not know was there.

When he died he left the land to his son, who,
also being ignorant, sold the field.

The man who bought it found the gold while ploughing
and was able to grant loans at a fair rate of interest.

He who has known this world and become wealthy,
let him disown it.

The earth and heavens may turn back before you,
but he who is truly alive won't know fear or death.

He who finds himself to be of this world is unfit.

Pity the body that leans upon the soul;
pity the soul that leans upon the flesh."

His disciples enquired,
"On what day will the Kingdom come?"

Lord Jesus replied, "It won't come through anticipation;
they won't say, 'Look, it's here, or look over there.'

The Kingdom of Heaven covers the Earth with glory,
but mankind fails to see it!"

Simon Peter said to the Lord and his disciples,
"Let Mary leave us,
because women are unfit for the Life Everlasting."

Jesus replied, "Wait, I'll guide her soul,
to make her as a real man,
in that place which transcends
the differences between the sexes,
so she'll become a living spirit.

For each woman who makes herself male in this way
and overcomes all differences
will enter the Kingdom of Heaven!"

THE GOSPEL OF
MARY MAGDALENE

Originally written in Greek, the Gospel of Mary Magdalene tells the disciples about Mary's unique revelations through her relationship with Jesus. Andrew and Peter question her veracity and ask why a woman should become a favourite disciple. They are admonished by Levi.

Mary questioned her Master,
"At the end of an aeon, will all matter be destroyed?"

Jesus answered,
"All of nature, its forms and creatures are interrelated;
all will be returned to their original source.

The essence of matter also returns
to the source of its own nature.
He who has ears, let him comprehend!"

Peter said, "As you've told us almost everything,
tell us this also: what is the world's sin?"

Jesus replied, "There is no sin in reality!

It is you who create sin, when you do deeds,
such as adultery, that are called sinful.

That's why Good enters your heart
to return you back to your source.

This is why you get ill and eventually die;
he who understands, let him understand.

Matter caused powerful passions to enter into you,
forces which come from its opposites in nature.

Then a sickness arises in the body; so be of strong faith!
If you're weak, gather strength in the presence of Nature;
he who has ears to hear, let him hear!"

Then Jesus greeted them saying, "Peace be with you all.
Take my peace into your Selves; be watchful so nobody leads
you astray claiming 'Look there, look here for the son of man.'

I tell you that the son of man is within you all!
Seek him inside; those who search diligently
and earnestly shall surely find him.

Then leave and preach the truth of the Kingdom
to those with ears to hear;
don't invent rules beyond those I've given.

Don't make laws like law-makers do
or else you'll be held back."
After he had said this he left.

The disciples were upset. They complained,
"How can we go to the Gentiles and preach the truth
of the Kingdom of the Son of Man?
If they won't save him, how will they save us?"

Then Mary rose and said, "Don't grieve! Be brave;
his grace is always with you to guard you.

Let's praise his magnitude; he's prepared us
and turned us into real men and women!"

When Mary said this she lifted their hearts up to the Good;
they started to study his words.

Peter said to Mary, "Dear sister,
we know our Saviour loves you
more than the rest of women.
Tell us his words that you remember,
those we've never heard before."

Mary answered, "What's concealed from you I'll tell;
I saw him in a vision and I told him.

He said, 'Blessed are you that your strength
wasn't shaken by my appearance,
for where the heart is lies buried treasure.'

I asked, 'Lord, does he or she who sees the vision
perceive it through soul or spirit?'

He answered, 'One perceives through neither soul nor spirit
but by mind, which mediates between both;
visions are mental.'

I pondered. 'I never saw you descend, now I see you ascend.
Why does my mind deceive me since you are part of me?'

My soul answered, 'But you didn't recognise me;
I serve you as your robe but you don't know me.'
When the voice ended I rejoiced inwardly.

When I came to ponder on ignorance, the third dark power,
it questioned my soul saying, 'Where are you heading?
You're enslaved by evil, so don't judge me.'

My soul replied, 'Why judge me; I haven't judged you.
I was imprisoned, although I never imprisoned.
I wasn't recognised, but I've known that All is being destroyed,
both in earth and heaven.'

When my soul had conquered ignorance it rose up
and saw the fourth power, which assumes seven forms.

The first is darkness, the second desire, then ignorance,
fear of death, power of the flesh, foolish reason,
and self-righteous pedantry.

These are the powers of anger and doubt; they ask,
'From where did you come, killer of men;
where are you heading, slayer of space?'

My soul replied, 'What bound me is dead,
what enveloped me has been vanquished;
my desires are over and ignorance is no more.

In this life I was freed from the world
and the chains of forgetfulness.
From now on I will rest in the eternal now;
for this age, this aeon, and in stillness.'"

Then Mary was silent,
for this was the truth Jesus had revealed.

Andrew then spoke, "Say what you like
about what Mary has said,
but I don't believe Jesus would tell us such strange notions!"

Peter said, "Did he really speak with Mary, a woman,
without our knowing? Are we to listen to her?
Did he favour her more than us?"

Then Mary cried to Peter, "My brother, do you believe
I made this up, or that I would lie about Jesus?"

Levi admonished Peter, "You've always been quick to anger;
now I see you doubting a woman as worthy as Mary.

Who do you think you are to dispute her testimony,
like an enemy? If Jesus made her upright,
who are we to disown her? Jesus knew her well;
that's why he loved her more than us.

Let's be penitent and don the robe of the perfect man
and make him one with ourselves, as he taught.

Let's proclaim his word, not make more laws
beyond those he ordered!"

The disciples then disbanded and began to teach his Gospel.

MELCHIZEDEK

An Apocalyptic Gospel, originally written in Greek, telling
of the visions received from celestial beings by the legendary
Melchizedek. It contains prophecies concerning the death, ministry
and resurrection of Jesus and the heretics who will deny him.

"I speak about Jesus, Son of God, who came
from the Aeon that speaks about all Aeons
and their nature; so I may be fit to adorn the robe
of love and righteousness.

At the end, my fellow Brethren, he unveiled
the truth in wise sayings and parables.

Death quaked and was enraged by itself and its Archons,
the dark powers, male and female gods,
archangels, and Earth's rulers.

Christ revealed the secret mysteries
but legalists soon dug his grave; they condemned him
as irreverent, unlawful and defiled.

On the third day he raised himself from the dead,
and as Saviour unveiled the truth that gives Life to the All.

Those in heaven conferred with those in the world
and the underworld about what would happen in his Name.

They would say he's unborn, though he's born;
that he doesn't eat or drink, though he does;
that he's uncircumcised, though he is;
that he's bodiless, though he has form;
that he didn't suffer, though he did;
that he wasn't resurrected, though he was!"

"All the tribes of the nations will learn truth
from you, Melchizedek, Great High Priest,
teacher of Abraham, the Prophet,
about his promise for a perfect, fulfilled life."

"I am also the Gamaliel, sent to
visit the people of Seth's offspring,
who are above all Aeons and their essence.

I acclaim Jesus Christ, Son of God,
who visited Abel Baruch
that you might hear this truth from me;
opposing forces are unaware of him and their own death.

I am here to tell these secrets, unveiled for the Brethren.
He shared the Living Truth with your children;
he offered them up as a sacrifice to the All.

But it isn't oxen you should offer for sins of infidelity,
nescience and evil deeds, for they don't reach
the Father of the All, but firm faith is certain
for those baptised in the waters that lie above.

So welcome that baptism which is approaching,
as they pray for the children of the Archons,
angels, and my Father's seed.

From which were born gods, angels, men,
nature, the heavens, the world, underworlds,
and the enigma of the feminine.

Yet what we're told isn't the real
meaning of Adam and Eve;
when they ate from the Tree of Knowledge,
they stamped hard on the Cherubim and Seraphim,
Earth's lords and Archons, their children,
and the secret male and female qualities in all nature.

But they denounced the Archons for they were fit
to receive the sacred immortal light!

But I'll keep silent, for we are the Brethren
who descended from the seed of Adam, Abel, Enoch,
Noah and myself, named Melchizedek.

These who are elected will never be condemned,
whether they're born from enemies, friends,
strangers, relations, reverent or irreverent.

All opposing forces, seen or unseen, in the world,
underworld or the heavens, will wage war.

I as Saviour will conquer,
and those chosen will surmount all;
not by words alone but through God's
grace will we end spiritual death.

I was ordered to unveil these secrets,
but don't tell anyone unless it's ordained
that you should do so."

Suddenly this High Priest Melchizedek praised God,
saying, "We must be grateful while He is living through us!

His grace is boundless. He has great compassion,
sending his angel of light from the Aeons,
to unveil the way to end ignorance and to lead us
from death to Eternal Life.

I am Melchizedek, High Priest of our God Supreme!
I know I am the similitude of Lord Jesus Christ,
the truest High Priest of God, sent to this Earth.

It's not a trifling matter that Almighty God is with us
and His angels that dwell in the world.

I speak of the Great Sacrifice that deceived Spiritual Death!
When Christ the Saviour died, he linked his own sacrifice
with the tendencies that are leading the people away,
the devilish demons of desire.

I offer myself to you as a child of this sacrifice,
together with all those who're mine.

To you, your own Self, the Father of the All,
and those you cherish, who've advanced through you
and are awakened and alive.

As decreed by the Flawless Law I shall speak my Name,
as I receive everlasting baptism from the living waters. Amen!

Sacred are you, Father of All, who exists
yet doesn't exist, eternally; holy are you,
Abel Baruch and Barbelo, Mother of Aeons,
and Doxomedon, first born of the Aeons,
Harmozel, the first Aeon,

Oriael, Daviethel, Eleleth and Mirochierothetou,
Chieftains of the Aeonic Light,
and my Self as Jesus Christ, eternal.

Blessed be my testimony; I speak now to end fear
and all that's connected with it,
that sphere of darkness in which bleak voices
and pains manifest, clothed with dread.

They spoke to me and said, 'Melchizedek,
we've been led astray from worship, faith and prayer.

We're of your primal stock, yet didn't heed
your priesthood, having heard the wiles of Satan,
who exists in this Aeon and seduces mankind.'

I, Melchizedek, answered, 'As your Saviour,
I cast Satan down so that you could
all be saved, yet you crucified me;
but as a corpse, from three on sabbath eve
'til nine, I rose from the dead.'

I was welcomed by my Father, who said,
'Be brave Melchizedek,
once high priest of the Archons.

Your foes that declared war,
you're victorious over them!
You've vanquished them.

Don't reveal this to anyone still identified
physically with their body,
unless it is commanded that you do so!'"

When the 'Brethren of the Rebirth of Life'
heard this great message they were transported
to realms high above the heavens!

THE GOSPEL
OF PHILIP

An early Greek, Valentinian collection of Jesus's sayings to his
disciples. Many refer to the profound sacramental mysteries
of Baptism, Anointment, the Eucharist and the Bridal Chamber.

A slave yearns to be free
but he doesn't hope to inherit his Master's house.

A boy isn't only a son,
but in time will lay claim to his father's estate.

Those who crave to be heirs of the dead
are already spiritually dead and will inherit death.

Those who seek to be heirs of the living are spiritually alive
and will inherit what is both alive and dead.

The dead inherit nothing, yet if they inherit what is living,
they'll gain Eternal Life.

A true Christian never dies for he has not lived in vain,
to inherit spiritual death.

He who has great faith in Truth has found the Real Life;
this man dares dying to his own Self, to be truly alive.

Since Lord Jesus Christ came the world has been recreated,
cities established, the dead buried.

When we were Jews we were fatherless
and had only an earthly mother.
Now, as Christians, we enjoy both the heavenly Father
and the divine Mother.

Those who sow in the hard winter reap in glorious summer.
This world is a harsh winter; summer is the eternal realm.
Let us sow now, in this wintry world,
so we may harvest in the splendid summer.

It is unworthy to pray for boons in this winter.
Wait, for the summer that will follow.

If a fool harvests in winter he'll tear out the good he has
and be like a barren Sabbath;
Christ came to hold some in debt
and to release others from usury.

Those who were exiled, he ransomed and made his own,
to set them apart; he pledged them according to his Will.

When he came, he willingly sacrificed his life,
for it had already been determined,
before this world was created.

He came first to redeem it as it had been pledged.
It had fallen into the hands of devilish demons
and was imprisoned;
but he came to save both the wicked and the good.

Light and darkness, life and death,
right and left, are inseparable twins.

For the good are not wholly good
nor the wicked wholly wicked,
nor is life merely life, nor death merely death;
each will return to its primal source.

But those who transcend these apparent opposites are eternal;
worldly names are full of deceit and delude our minds.

They muddy the distinction between right and wrong
with words like father, spirit, son, life, light,
resurrection and church.
In the eternal world there are no such deceptions.

One Name is never uttered,
the Name the Father gave His Son.
For the Son couldn't have become the Father
unless he knew His Name.

Those who know this Name never speak it.
Truth brought names into being for our sake.

The dark powers wanted to deceive man,
to confuse his relationship with the truly good.
They took good names and gave them to the bad,
so that with these names they might bind them.

But through grace they remove them from the bad
and restore them to the good; these dark forces
wished to steal man's freedom and enslave him.
These powers obstruct man's salvation,
for if man is saved, animal sacrifice would end.

Before Christ there was no manna.
Just as Eden had many fields to feed flocks
but no wheat to feed Man.

Man used to munch like the beasts, but Christ,
the perfect Man, brought manna from heaven
so Mankind could be fed by the spirit.

The dark powers imagine it is by their own self will
that they do what they do; yet the Holy Spirit
secretly does all through them, as it wills.

Truth which lives since the beginning is sown everywhere;
many see the sowing, few know the reaping.

Some claim that Mary's conception was immaculate.
They're mistaken; women cannot conceive
from the Holy Spirit, which is feminine.
It means that Mary wasn't defiled by dark powers,
which defile themselves.

Jesus said to his disciples,
"Bring gifts to your Father's house;
don't steal from there."

Jesus is our Lord's secret name, Christ is his revealed name.
In Syriac it is Messiah.
The Nazarene is he who reveals the hidden.

Those who claim our Lord first died then ascended, are wrong!
He ascended, then died.

No one hides a precious jewel in a large container,
but often we have thrown many things into
a small worthless box.

The soul is precious, but not its flesh;
some fear they'll rise up naked and wish to ascend fully robed,
but they don't see that those clothed only by flesh
are naked and ashamed.

In Corinthians it states:
"Flesh and blood shall not inherit the Kingdom."
What cannot inherit is the body alone; what will inherit
is that which belongs to Jesus and his holy communion.

In John's Gospel, Jesus says, "He who will not eat my flesh
and drink my blood has no life in him."
His flesh is the Word, his blood is the Holy Spirit.
He who receives these has real food, drink and clothes.

It is necessary to ascend through the Word of God,
for All is contained in that.

In this world those with clothes are better than those in rags;
in the Kingdom of Heaven God's robes are superior
to the souls that wear them.

It is through fire and water that the world is purified:
the visible by the invisible, the open by the hidden.

Much is hidden in the visible: water in flowers,
fire in baptismal oil and balsam.

Jesus won them by cunning
for he did not appear as he really was
but in a form that they could see.

To the great he seemed great, to the little he was little,
to the angels he was an angel, to men he was a man.
So his Word was hidden from all; some indeed saw him
and imagined they were seeing themselves.

When he came to his disciples in splendid glory
on the Mount of Olives he wasn't small;
he became great and made his disciples great
so they could see him in his greatness.

On that day he said in gratitude,
"You who have united perfect light with holy spirit,
unite us with the angels as well.

Don't scorn the Lamb;
without him it's impossible to know the King.
No one may visit the King without robes of light.

The Heavenly Man has many more sons than the earthly;
Adam's sons soon die, but the sons of the Perfect Man
don't die, and are ever reborn.

The Father creates a son,
but the son hasn't the power to create another.
He who has been reborn is unable to bestow regeneration,
so the son wins brothers but not sons.

All men and women in this world are born naturally,
but those reborn in God are nurtured by heaven.
It is by the divine kiss of grace that the Perfect are reborn;
we also embrace each other to aid conception
by one another's grace."

Three walked with Christ: Mary, his mother;
her sister, also Mary; and Mary Magdalene.
All three were called Mary.

Father and son are single names, omnipresent,
above and below; in the concealed and the revealed
the Holy Spirit is dual: it is in the revealed below
and in the concealed above.

Some holy men are served by sinister powers,
deceived by a spirit into the belief
that they're serving an ordinary man.

A disciple asked Jesus for something from this world.
He answered, "Ask your mother.
She'll bring you things which belong to another."

The apostles said to the disciples,
"May our sacrifices contain salt!"
They called Sophia, the Divine Wisdom, "salt".
Without "the savour of salt", no sacrifice will be acceptable.
Sophia is childless, so she is termed a "grain of salt".

Wherever they manifest in their own path,
the Holy Spirit and her offspring will be fecund.
What the Father owns, He gives to the son
when he arrives at manhood.

Those who've fallen away, yet are reborn by the spirit,
may drift because of the spirit.
So by the same exhalation, fire blazes and is extinguished.

Echamoth means wisdom of death;
one who knows death is termed "the lesser wisdom".

There are tame beasts like cattle, mules, dogs and sheep,
but wild beasts live mainly in the desert.

Man ploughs his field with the aid of the ox,
and from tame beasts he's fed.

The Perfect Man ploughs through his subdued powers,
preparing for all to come into Being.
Thus the world is established

through good and evil, right and left.

The Holy Spirit shepherds us and rules all powers:
tame, wild and unique.
He hedges us in so we cannot stray.

Adam was created to be beautiful, but Cain was not worthy.
Adultery followed murder; he was the snake's child.

God is a Master Dyer, His good and true dyes
dissolve with the robes they dye.

His dyes are immortal by means of His colours;
first, He dips with water.

It's impossible to see what exists,
unless one becomes similar.

But the worldly man sees the sun without being a sun;
the same with heaven and earth.

If you know the Spirit you become the Spirit;
if you know Christ you become Christ-like;
if you know the Father you become as the Father.

The worldly see the All but fail to know their own Self;
through Truth you learn to know your Self;

what you know you become.

Faith accepts, love bestows.
None can receive without great faith.
No one can truly give without love;
he doesn't seek gain from what he gives.

He who has received something
other than our Lord remains a Jew.

The apostles prior to ourselves had names for him.
Jesus was first the Nazarean,
then Christ, and then the Messiah.

Messiah means both Christ and "the measured";
Jesus means "redemption", Nazarene "the truthful".
Both the Nazarene and Jesus have been justly measured.

If a pearl falls into mud it becomes dirty and spoiled,
but if it is washed in balsam oil it becomes precious;
yet it is always valued in the sight of its owner.

The Sons of God, wherever they may be,
are also valued by their Father.
If you say "I'm a Jew," no one's impressed;
if you say "I'm a Roman," no one's depressed.
If you say you're a Greek, a barbarian,

a slave or a freeman, no one's worried.

But if you say "I'm a Christian,"
people will quake with fear.
Would I were like that person
whose name they cannot bear to hear.

God consumes man, egos are sacrificed before Him;
animals were sacrificed to those who weren't God.

Glass goblets and pottery jugs are both formed by fire;
if glass breaks it can be re-moulded,
but clay vessels are shattered,
for they came into being without breath.

A mule that turned a mill stone walked a hundred leagues,
but when released it was still on the same spot!
There are folk who make pilgrimages without progress.

When dusk falls they see neither city nor town,
man-made monuments nor sights of nature,
powers nor angels; fools suffer in vanity.

Jesus is the Eucharist;
in Syriac he's called Pharisatha,
"the one who is stretched out";
Jesus came to nail this world to the Cross!

Jesus entered Levi's dye works;
he took seventy-two dyes
and threw them in the vat.

The cloths all emerged pure white.
He said, "The Son of Man comes as a dyer."

The childless Wisdom is mother of angels.
Of all his disciples he loved his companion,
Mary Magdalene, the most, and kissed her.

The disciples asked, "Why do you love her most?"
He answered, "When a blind and sighted man
are both in darkness, they are equal.

When light dawns, he who can see will know the light;
he who is blind will stay in the dark."

Jesus said, "Blessed be he who IS, before he came into being,
for he who IS has always been and always shall be."

Man's mastery is invisible, and lies in the concealed.
So he controls animals who are stronger
in terms of the visible; thus they survive.
But when he leaves, they quarrel and fight,
kill one another and become cannibals.

Now they can all eat because
a superior man has tilled the ground.

If someone dives deep into the well of living water
and surfaces empty handed, saying, "I am a Christian,"
he has only borrowed the name with interest.

If he receives the Holy Spirit, His Name is the gift.
He who accepts this gift doesn't have to give it back,
but from those who borrow at interest,
payment is demanded.

This is the way this mystery is experienced.
Marriage is also a great mystery!
Without it our world couldn't continue;
contemplate this relationship.

Marriage in imagination and fantasy is a defilement.
Forms of demonic spirits are male and female;
males unite with souls that dwell in the female form
of those who are disobedient.

None can escape them,
for they delay those who do not receive
the male and female powers of bride and groom.
They are received from the reflected light
of the bridal chamber.

When a loose woman sees a lone man,
she leaps on him to defile him.
Similarly, lechers, when they see a lone beauty,
they seduce, to defile.
But if man and wife are seen together,
the female cannot seize the man
nor can the man enter the woman.

So if this symbol and an angel are united,
nothing harmful can penetrate man or woman.

He who is no longer "of the world" cannot be delayed
on the grounds that "he was once in the world".

He is obviously beyond the plagues of lust and fear;
he masters the mind and senses and is above jealousy.
If the enemy comes to attack,
he'll be defeated by a higher power.

There are some who claim to be faithful,
just to vanquish impure thoughts and feelings.
But if they're firm in the Holy Spirit,
nothing unclean can ever touch them.

Don't be afraid of the body, but don't adore it.
If you fear, it will gain mastery;
if you adore, it will render you helpless.

So the pilgrim lives in the world,
in regeneration, or in between.

God prevent me from falling in between two places;
there is spiritual death.

In the world there's good and evil;
its goodness is not wholly good,
nor is its evil wholly evil.
But there's an evil that is diabolic,
this "in betweenness".

While in the world,
it is worthy to seek and find regeneration,
so that when we leave the body we are at peace
and not left hanging in the middle.

Many stray from the straight path;
be wise and don't "be of this world"
before you sin.

There are some who are impotent
in their will to act and procrastinate;
they miss the mark.

An apostle, in a vision, saw many folk trapped in a fire.
The voice of the Lord offered to save them;

they disbelieved, hesitated, and all perished in the flames.

It's from fire and water that spirit and soul come into Being.
It is from these elements, and light,
that the groom of the bridal chamber comes to be.
The fire is the baptismal anointing oil.
The light's form is white, bright and beautiful.

Truth does not come into the world without robes;
it enters through words and pictures.
Truth cannot be received by the world in any other way.

There is rebirth and an image of rebirth.
We are born again through the image of "Resurrection".
The bridal chamber is the image of "Regeneration".

Those who speak the names of the Father,
the Son and the Holy Spirit, do so for you.

If we do not know them in the heart,
the name "Christian" will be removed.

But we receive the boundless grace of the power of his cross.
This power the apostles called right and left;
it transforms men from mere Christians into a Christ.

The Lord performed all his acts in mystery: baptism,

communion, redemption, and in the bridal chamber.
He said, "I came to make the below as the above,
the outside as the inside, and to unite them all through
the Word and the symbol."

Those who claim, "There's the heavenly man,
and one above him" are wrong.
There are two heavenly men: one revealed, who is below,
and one who owns the hidden, who is above.

It is better to say "internal and external
and what's outside the external".
That is the reason our Lord called destruction
the "outer darkness".

He said, "Enter the chamber of your heart,
seal the door then pray to your Father who is in secret."

The Father is the one within them all and is the perfection.

There's nothing else beyond "That I am".

Before Christ, some came from where they couldn't enter;
if they did go in, they couldn't exit.

Those who entered, Christ released;
those who came out, he returned.

When Adam was still with Eve there was no death;
after separation death appeared.

If a man or woman regains his or her former Self,
there'll be an end to death.

"My God, my God. Oh Lord, why have you forsaken me?"
Jesus pronounced these words on the cross as a mystery,
quoting from King David's Psalms.

The bridal chamber is not fit for beasts,
slaves and loose women.
It is for free men and the virginal.

By the Holy Spirit and Christ,
we're born again, through both;
we're baptised by the Spirit and,
when reborn, made One.

You cannot see your reflection
in a glass or pool without light.

Nor can you see reflected light
without a mirror or water,
so it is right to baptise in light and water.
The light is the oil.

In Jerusalem there were three temples for the sacrifice.
The one facing west was named "Holy",
the south-facing temple was the "Holy of the Holy",
the east-facing one the "Holy of Holies",
where only the High Priest was allowed.

Baptism is the Holy,
Redemption is the Holy of the Holy;
the Holy of the Holies is the bridal chamber.

Baptism contains redemption and resurrection;
redemption happens in the bridal chamber.

The veil was lifted so some below could rise above.
Dark powers cannot see those robed in Perfect Light.
They cannot be impeded by them.
We are enrobed sacramentally in this light by atonement.

If the female did not divorce the male
she would not die with the male;
his exile is the advent of death.
Christ came to heal this alienation.

The bride is reunited with her groom in the bridal chamber
and can never be divorced again.

Eve separated from Adam because they were not united

in the bridal chamber at the heart's core.
Adam's soul came into Being through the breath of the spirit.
The mother was given, his soul was taken
and the spirit granted;
linked to spirit he spoke words beyond comprehension.

Dark powers were envious for they had missed the chance
to enter the wedding chamber.

Jesus came to the River Jordan
in the perfection of the Kingdom of Heaven,
conceived before the All and reborn anew.

Anointed, he anointed afresh;
redeemed, he redeemed his flock.

I must speak about the great mystery;
The Father of All married a virgin, who descended,
and fire glowed upon their wedding day.

His visible body, the whole universe,
came into Being on that day.
He left the bridal chamber as one who
came into being from groom and bride.
So Jesus established all through these miracles.

It is best for each disciple to abide in his peace.

Adam came into being from two virgins:
the Spirit and the Earth.

Christ's birth came to heal the evil from the Fall.
Two trees grow in Eden: one bears beasts, the other mankind.
Adam ate from the tree of beasts.

He became like an animal, so his offspring worshipped them.
Men make gods and praise their creation.
What a man achieves depends on his talents, and his children.
They commence in ease, but man is made in the image of
strength yet has children with ease.

In this world slaves serve the free;
in heaven, the free will minister to slaves.

Children of the bridal chamber
minister to the children of their marriage.
The name of these offspring is peace.

They don't need form because they have meditation;
they are abundant in their Glory.

Those who enter living waters will bless them in his Name.

Jesus said, "So we shall fulfil all righteousness."

Those who say they'll die first
and then rise again are mistaken.

If they do not receive resurrection while alive,
they'll receive nothing when they die.

I, Philip the Apostle, said,
"Joseph planted a forest because he needed wood.

He made a cross from his trees;
his son was crucified on that cross.
But the Tree of Life is at the heart of that forest.

We press baptismal oil from the olive,
and resurrection follows.

The world is a corpse eater consuming dead animals;
all who eat that meat also die.

Truth is a Life consumer;
no one who feeds upon it will die.
Jesus brought such food.

The Garden of Eden is the place where angels say,
'Eat this and don't eat that, as you so desire.'
Where I eat, all is from the Tree of Knowledge.
It destroyed Adam but can now bring men back from death.

The Tree is the Law.
It's empowered to give knowledge of good and evil.
It neither removes evil nor establishes good,
but kills those who choose disobediently.

God said, 'Eat this, don't eat that,' and death was begun.

The chrism, the oil of holy unction,
is superior to the ceremony of baptism itself.
The word Christian is derived
from chrism and the name Christ.

The Father anointed the Son;
the Son anointed the apostles, who anointed us.
He who has been anointed owns the resurrection,
the light, the cross and the Holy Spirit.

The Father anointed the Son
in the bridal chamber of the heart's core;
the Son surrendered his will.

The Father was in the Son and the Son in the Father.
This is the Kingdom."

Jesus said, "Some have entered baptism
and the kingdom laughing, as if it was of little worth,
so, out they come."

The world came through error,
for the Creator wished it to be immutable and immortal.

It failed to reach His aim;
things cannot be immutable but His Sons are;
no one can become immutable
without first becoming His Son.
But he who is unable to receive cannot give.

The grail contains water and wine, consecrated as His blood,
for which we give thanks.
It is filled with Holy Spirit and is from the perfect man;
when we drink we receive His perfection.

The living water is His body. We must don the living man;
before we bathe in the living waters we must strip bare
so we can wear the perfect man.

Horses sire horses, men sire men, God sires a god.
Compare that with groom and bride
who come from the chamber.

There's no real Jew, but from Judaism came Christianity;
these are the Chosen, the sons of man,
known in the world as the children of the bridal chamber
so they may endure for life everlasting!

In this life, marriage between husband and wife
shows strength offset by physical frailty;
in the eternal sphere the form is not the same.

They are not separate; both come from the one
strong enough to rise above the heart of flesh.

It is needed to own the All, to know one's Self.
If one doesn't know one's Self
it's impossible to enjoy what's owned;
those who've come to know themselves
enjoy what they own.

The ignorant will be unable to delay
the perfect man or see him.
To attain the right to enter the Kingdom
one must be adorned with his Light.

The true priest is totally holy,
for he has consecrated the bread;
by enlivening the water of baptism
Jesus rid man of death.

If we descend to those living waters,
we do not descend to death;
then we will not be recycled into the world's spirit.
When this spirit blows it brings a harsh winter;

when the Holy Spirit breathes, glorious summer blooms.

He who knows the Truth is free from sin,
but he who sins is its slave.

Truth is the mother, knowledge the father;
those whom the world believes to be sinless are free.

Knowledge of Truth can make people proud;
real freedom is being free from arrogance.

Love builds, but he who is free often becomes her servant,
through love, of slaves, unable to reach Truth.

Love never controls; it doesn't claim this is "yours"
and this is "mine" but says, "All is yours!"

Spiritual love is wine and perfume;
if those anointed come with bad-smelling ointment,
then they should leave.

The good Samaritan gave wine and oil to the weak man;
his ointment healed because love cures a multitude of sins.

A mother's child looks like her husband, if he truly loves her;
if he or she cheats, the child resembles one of their defilers.
If the wife sleeps with her husband

but thinks only of her lover,
the child will look like him.

You who dwell with God's Son, don't adore the world
but love the Lord so your offspring will be like Him
and not the world.

Man enjoys sex with a woman, the stallion with a mare,
the bull with a cow; so spirit mingles with spirit,
reason weds reason, light shares light.

If you're born a man or a woman, a human being will love you;
if you become truly spiritual, the spirit will love you.
If you become one with He who dwells above,
saints in heaven will kneel down before you.

If you become a beast, outside and below the spiritual realm,
neither human, spirit, reason nor light will love you;
the Spirit within, and above, won't dwell in you;
you'll lose your Friend.

He who subdues his personal will shall become free.

He who becomes free by grace of his master,
but then barters himself back
to hard slavery of his personal will,
won't ever be free again.

If you're a farmer you need earth, rain, wind and sun;
God as your Farmer requires you to cultivate faith,
hope, love and Self Knowledge.
Faith is our fertile ground; hope, our gentle rain;
love, the soft breeze; Self Knowledge, the sunshine!
Grace descends to earth from heaven.

Blessed is the one who saved souls; that one is Christ.
He came to earth and unburdened all
who had faith in him, the perfect man.
The Word of God tells us the Saviour is beyond description;
No one else can achieve so much, or comfort so many.

He comforts all, never causing sorrow
to those who take refuge in Him alone;
wickedness and guile cause distress.
The perfect man brings peace and love,
yet some are stressed by that notion.

There was once a farmer who owned sons, slaves,
cattle, dogs, swine, corn, barley, grass and nuts.
He was a caring man; he gave bread to children,
corn meal to slaves, bones to dogs, acorns to pigs.

So it is with God's disciples;
bodily appearances won't mislead them.
They'll scrutinise each other's spiritual

condition and advise appropriately.

There are animals in human form;
when He sees what they are He feeds them the right diet.
To slaves He gives basic lessons,
to children, detailed guidance.

Our Lord is the Son of Man
and his son is he who creates through Him;
The Son of Man can also give birth;
to create a creature, to give birth to offspring.
He who creates strives for all to see;
He who brings rebirth toils in private and is concealed.

Only a man and wife can tell when they enjoy sex.
Marriage is a mystery;
if there's mystery in the wedlock of impurity,
how much more mystery is there
in the purity of the bridal chamber?

The sacred marriage is not carnal;
it is without desire and subject to God's will,
not from darkest night but from brightest light.

When sex goes public, it's prostitution.
The bride can play the whore, to be defiled by a lecher
if she leaves the bedroom and is seen.

Let the true wife confide only in her parents,
and friends and family of the groom;
they are permitted to enter the bridal chamber.

The rest must pray only to hear her voice
and enjoy the perfume of her ointment;
let them feed from table crumbs like puppies.

Brides and grooms belong to the chamber;
no one should see them together until they're like them.

Abraham was circumcised, teaching that it is
right to admonish the flesh.

Providing man's inner parts are protected,
they'll labour and live; once exposed, they'll stop!
If a man's intestines are opened up, he'll die.

The same with a tree.
While the root is covered, it will shoot and grow;
if it's exposed, the tree will wither.
It is so with all birth in this world.

If the root of wickedness lies hidden in the dark
it waxes strongly; when exposed to the light
of awareness it perishes.

That is why Matthew writes,
"Already the axe is laid at the root of the trees";
it will not only cut the trunk but also sever the root.
Jesus pulled up the root of worldly sinfulness;
prophets partly did his work.

Each one of us must dig down deep within ourselves
and find the root of this evil egotism in the heart,
so it will perish.

If we ignore this root, more poisonous fruit
is produced in the heart;
it becomes our task master and enslaves us,
forcing us to do what it desires.

It is powerful until seen and is active;
ignorance is the mother of all evil;
It will end in death!
For those who come from this,
iniquity will cease to exist.

When all the Truth is revealed then man may be perfected.
Truth, unlike ignorance, while latent is at rest,
but when revealed is stronger than the foe.
It brings freedom!
John wrote, "Truth will set you free."
Ignorance is slavery, Self knowledge is liberation.

If we know Truth, its blossom will flower in
our hearts and bring salvation;
at the moment we're a mere appearance in creation.

We say that the strong are held in respect as great people
and the reviled are the weak, who are despised;
but the truth is different and revealed in a symbol.
The bridal chamber is concealed; it is the holy in the Holy.

The bridal veil hides how God commands His work;
when unveiled, this house will be destroyed.

The Godhead will retire, not to the Holy of Holies
for it will not mingle with the pure light
and flawless perfection.
It will rest beneath the arms of the cross;
an ark will be their refuge
when the deluge descends.

The true priests may enter within the veil
with the high priest;
the veil was not open only at the top
for then it would be closed to those below.
It was not open only at the bottom
for then it would be closed to those above.
It was open from top to bottom.
Those above revealed to those below,

so we could know the mysteries of Truth.

Truth is what is held in great respect and is really strong!
We enter bowed in weakness;
we are humble compared with God's great power and glory.
His power and glory surpass all power and glory.

Divine perfection is revealed
with the concealed secrets of Truth.
The Holy of Holies opens;
we are invited to the bridal chamber.

Hidden wickedness is now less effective,
but not cleansed from the seed of the Spirit;
many may still be slaves of evil.

When revealed, the perfect light will shine on all;
all those within its rays will be anointed
and receive baptism of the chrism.
The slaves shall be free and the prisoners redeemed!

Matthew wrote, "Every plant my Father in Heaven
has not planted shall be plucked."

The exiled will return to unity and be fulfilled.

All who enter the bridal chamber will light the light
as at night weddings.

But the mysteries of the marriage are perfected by day,
not at night; an eternal day that never sets.

All who become sons of the bridal chamber
will receive the light;
they'll be invisible and free from torment, even in this world.

When he departs, he'll have known Truth
through these symbols;
The world has become Eternal, and is perfect for him.

This is how truth is given; not hidden in darkest night
but revealed in brightest day of holy light!

POIMANDRĒS

OR THE POWER AND WISDOM OF GOD

A famed Gnostic work by the legendary Hermes Trismegistus. After an Angelic Revelation, he describes the mysteries of Creation, the Destiny of Man and the Soul. The Tract concludes with an important Gnostic Sermon and a devotional Prayer.

From The Hermetica Tract I

Once, while meditating on "what is", my soul soared,
my senses stood firm, like those of a man drunk with sleep,
from too much food and physical exertion.

A huge Being of limitless size appeared,
called my name and said,
"What do you wish to hear, see, learn
and know from your comprehension?"

I asked, "Who are you?"

"I am Poimandrēs, Being of Kingship,
mind of Gnosis. I know all your needs,
I'm with you everywhere."

I replied, "I want very much to learn about life,
 its nature, and to know God."

He answered, "Remember all you care to know;
I shall teach you."

Suddenly he was transformed into brightest light.

From this vision, radiant, clear and joyful,
I felt wide open. I enjoyed this state.

After a time darkness descended, fearful and dense,
coiling serpent-like.
Then the darkness seemed to liquefy vigorously,
emitting grey smoke.

It roared unspeakably.

Then a voice like the crackle of fire spoke:
"Have you understood the meaning of your vision?"

"No doubt I'll come to know its meaning," I said.

"I am that Light, mind of Gnosis, and God.
'That' which was, before water issued from the night.

The illuminating Word that comes from Gnosis
is the son of God."

"Proceed," I said.

"What you need to know, is 'That' within you,
which sees and hears, and comes from God's Word.
Your Self is the Father,
they're not separate, their union is life."

I expressed my thanks for this revelation.

He continued to speak, "Understand and recognise
this Light behind and within your mind."

He then gazed into my eyes for some while.
I horripilated.

When he raised his head I saw the Light of numerous
powers and an infinitely radiant universe.
This fire, powerful yet restrained, was held in place.

I was terrified, but he addressed me once more.

"In your mind you've witnessed archetypal form:
the primordial, pristine principle that IS,
before birth and death."

"What about the natural elements?" I asked,
"How have they arisen?"

"From God's wisdom, which, absorbing the Word
and seeing the beauty of the potential,
actualised it, creating a universe
through its own elements and myriad souls.

This 'nous' which is God is androgyne,
being both life and light.

By so uttering, He gave birth to another mind,
a skilled craftsman, Lord of fire and spirit.

He created seven Lords, the planets who ruled
the sensual worlds.

Their government was called Destiny;
from the elements whose gravity plunges downwards.

The Word soared to create the skill of nature,
linking this craft with the craftsman.
This mind with the Word, drew whirling circles,

turning from an endless beginning to a beginningless end.

The circles created living creatures, animals and beasts.

From the wind flew winged birds of glorious plumage,
and insects with rainbow wings.
Water brought scaly fish and monsters of the deep.

Gnosis, Father of All, life and light, created Man,
whom He loved like His own son.
Man was fair, created in the image of his God.

Enamoured by His own form,
God granted him all His craft skills.

So the Father allowed man to exercise his power,
entering with permission the craftsman's sphere.

He learned well and yearned to break through
the outer ring of the spherical realms
and keep to the rule, of one given power over fire.

Thus having authority over the world of souls
and dumb animals, he pierced the vault
and peered through the cosmic framework,
revealing to lower nature God's fair form.

Nature laughed with love when she saw his beauty
and splendid energy.
In water she saw the reflection of his noble shape
and its shadow on the Earth.

When Man saw his form so mirrored, he fell into self love
and inhabited this imagination.

Nature then embraced her newly Beloved
with welcoming arms.

Thus man is twofold: mortal in body,
immortal in essence, subject to fate.

He's above the cosmic framework, yet is its slave.
He's tireless because he emanates from that One
who is indefatigable.

This is the mystery of Gnosis, kept secret until now.

When nature consummated her love with Man,
she bore seven babes, androgyne and exalted,
like the seven planetary Lords of the spheres."

Poimandrēs paused.
I interrupted and said, "Pray please continue,
I long to learn more!"

He replied, "Be quiet,
I've yet to complete my discourse.

I will tell you about her births.
Earth was feminine; oceans and rain fertilised her.
Fire was the force of maturation.

Nature took spirit from ether
and bore more bodies in man's form.

From Life and Light came soul and mind.
All things in the sensual worlds remained
until the cycle ceased.
When the cycle ended, the ties between all
were unfastened by Divine Wisdom.

Living beings were split into two halves, male and female.

But God ordered them to multiply
and to recognise their immortality.
And for many that desire
is the cause of their spiritual death.

Then providence ordained sexual intercourse,
so all creatures multiplied.

The one who recognised his true Self
reached the chosen Good.

But those still identified with the body from desire
transmigrated to the darkness of continuous rebirth."
I enquired what wrong they had committed,
that they were deprived of immortality.

He rebuked me, saying, "You talk like a fool
who doesn't reflect on what he's heard.
Try and consider why they deserve
this form of living death."

I answered, "Because what first appeared in each body
was dreaded darkness, born of the watery nature
from which death drinks."

"Yes, you've understood,
but why does this comprehension
lead a man towards God?"

I answered his question.
"Because the Father of All, being Light and Life,
made man in his own image."

"You are correct! Life and Light are God,
the Father from whom Man emanates.

So contemplate this well
and you too shall rise from the dead."

"However," I replied,
"God said the man who is mindful should Self remember.
But surely all people have a mind?"

He rebuked me sharply. "Hold your tongue.
Enough talk. Listen! I my Self,
I Am, ever present to the blessed,
good, pure, aware, compassionate, holy.

This Presence of the Self becomes an aid.
They soon apperceive this basic Recognition.

They worship their Father with love and gratitude,
praising and chanting hymns devotedly.

Before physical death they learn detachment
from the dire effects of lascivious lust.

I AM, as their Self, will not permit
these defects to harm them.

As their friend and door keeper
I forbid entry to those with shameful habits.
From these I keep due distance:

the evil, jealous, greedy, violent, irreverent.

Those who yield to this lust, a demon wounds
with burning coals and arms with pride
so greater vengeance may befall.

Such a victim never ceases craving carnal concupiscence,
suffering in darkness so he's tormented and the fire increases."

"You've taught me well. Please tell me more
about the Ascent, and how it happens."

He graciously replied, "In renouncing the gross body,
you hand yourself over to transformation
and the old form goes.

The wicked demon to whom you gave
your temperament becomes powerless.

The body's senses rise up and return to the Source,
separating and remingling with His original energy.

The old feelings and cravings return to irrational nature,
and the regenerated Man is reborn through the spheres.

At the first, he renounces getting and letting go;
at the second, evil inclination.

At the third, illusion and delusion.

At the fourth, his usurping, cardinal, egotistic arrogance.

At the fifth, wilful presumption and jeopardising bravado.

At the sixth, greed, avarice, miserliness,
springing from passion for wealth and perishable possessions.

At the seventh, all deceit, betrayal, guile,
and calumny, lurking in ambush.

Then, stripped naked of the old man,
he enters the sphere of Sophia, Divine Wisdom.

He has restored his own natural power,
and along with the Elect worships his Father.

All those present rejoice in His Presence.
And being His friend he finds powers beyond
this sphere, and praises God with a new song.

His hymn rises to his Father and he surrenders himself
to God's almighty will and enters into Him.
This is the ultimate Good of Self Knowledge.

Why do you hesitate?
Hasten and become a guide to the fit,
so mankind might share God's salvation."

As he was speaking he renewed himself
from the Source and sent me forward, empowered,
and informed on the universal nature and the supreme vision;
after I had given thanks to my Father of the All.

I then proclaimed to my fellow beings
the beauty of holiness and Self Knowledge.

"Oh, poor, blind people, who've seduced yourselves
by drunkenness, spiritual sloth and ignorance of God.

Sober up! Put an end to your evil malaise;
you're all hypnotised, as if in a lunatic dream."

When the people heard they gathered round,
and I repeated: "Why have you committed spiritual suicide
when your birthright is Eternal Life?

You who've flirted with crude lies
and partnered stupidity, reflect, repent!

Abandon corruption and degeneration.
Take your rightful place in immortality!"

Some, in the grip of death, moved on,
mocking and scoffing.

But those who yearned for enlightenment
prostrated themselves at my feet.

I then became their guide, teaching salvation.
And I sowed the seeds of higher wisdom,
And they drank from living waters.

When dusk fell I led them in praise of our Almighty God,
and they retired.

Within myself I acknowledged Poimandrēs' love,
and I rejoiced.

My body's sleep became my soul's temperance.
Closing my eyes became real vision;
my silence was filled with beatitude.
This happened because I had listened attentively
to his Word of Kingship.

I had arrived, inspired by the divine breath of Truth.

So I sing praises to the One God, with all my heart,
with all my soul and with all my might!

"Holy is God, Father of the All.
Seated in your own power, who yearns
to be known by his own children.

Who by your Word has created all things precisely as they are.

The whole of nature is your reflected image.

You're stronger than all forces, superior to all excellencies.
The Supreme Perfection!

We can only meet You in silence: the unspeakable,
unsayable, inscrutable, unknowable.

Accept our sacrifice of the hearts and souls
that cleave to You.

Grant my prayer, that I don't fail in the Self Knowledge
that befits my True Nature.

Give me the strength and I shall enlighten those
trapped in the snare of ignorance:
the brothers and sisters of my race,
Your sons and daughters!

This is my Faith.
I walk on victoriously to Life and Light.

Blessed are You my Father.
I am Your slave and wish to aid Your work of holiness,
since You've blessed me with great wisdom!"

THE APOCALYPSE
OF GREAT POWER

A n early Coptic Gnostic narrative telling of Creation, Divine Justice, Mercy and the conflict between Good and Evil. It concludes with a dramatic apocalyptic vision of the world's end and the salvation of Souls.

He who'll know our One Great Power
will not be seen.
Its fire won't kill him, but will purify
and burn up all his worldly goods.

All who see my shape shall be saved,
those from seven days
to one hundred and twenty years old.

I instructed some to collect all that's been revealed
as the book of our Great Power.
So that power may inscribe their name in its radiance
and their labour end.

That they may be purified, dispersed and self-abnegated,

so they may meet in that sphere where no one else can see.

But you can see me and make
your home in our Great Power.
Comprehend what's happened to Be,
so you can understand what endures
and what form the Aeon takes.

Why not enquire diligently into that?

Think how vast is the ocean, beyond measure
and comprehension, in beginning and end.
It maintains the world, and wafts the winds
where gods and angels dwell.

But for he who is above all this there's awe and light,
and to him my book is unveiled.

I have written it as a service for created human beings,
for it is impossible for any man to be firm
without knowing The One.

Nor can an Aeon endure without Him.
Only he who knows his own Self
can contemplate "That" in purity.

Know "That Spirit" and his heart.

He sacrificed himself for mankind
so they may receive perennial life;
since He possesses Life within Himself,
He's able to give it to all.

Then night and hell together conspired to steal my fire,
and this darkness will not return to those who are truly mine.

Its eyes cannot stand my Light;
after spirits and waters moved,
what was left came into being,
the entire Aeon of Creation and its forces.

Fire issued from them and the Power descended
in the middle of their energies and wished to see
my similitude, so the Soul became its duplicate.

This is the creation that came into existence;
before emerging, it was blind,
for the fleshly Aeon entered gross bodies
and they were granted length of days.

For when they self-corrupted and penetrated the flesh,
the fleshly father, water, revenged himself when he learnt
that Noah was saintly and fit, and that the fleshly father
keeps even the angels in servitude.

And Noah taught righteousness
for one hundred and twenty years,
and no one paid due attention
until he built an ark of teak
and his chosen flock took refuge.

When the flood descended, Noah and his sons were saved.
For if their ark hadn't been meant for man and his animals,
the deluge wouldn't have happened.

In this way Noah decided to rescue the gods,
angels and spiritual powers, their magnitude,
their manna and manner of living.
He moved from that Aeon and fed them in eternal realms.

The fleshly judgement was pronounced;
only the Creation of the Power remained.

The next Aeon was the small, psychic one,
which when mingled with the physical
gave birth in souls and polluted them.

Its offspring were rafts of wrath, jealousy, ill will, guile,
disdain, strife, mendacity, wicked advice, depression,
hedonism, lowliness, corruption, falsity, sickness,
bad judgement and depravity, all of which were craved
according to their particular pernicious lusts.

You who are fast asleep, dreaming the dream of life,
stir yourself, awaken and attentively search within!

Savour and enjoy true nourishment,
teach the Word of God from the fountain of life.
Put an end to wicked appetites,
yearning for Anomoean doctrine and wicked falsity
that lacks a firm foundation.

The Fire Mother was powerless;
she set light to the soul and the world,
scorching all its constructions.
Even its Arch-Mentor died.

And if there was nothing left to ignite,
she'd set light to herself and be bodyless,
incinerating gross matter until she removed all evil;
this is the psychic Aeon.

A man will appear who knows the Great Power;
he'll accept and understand me;
he'll drink his Mother's milk, preach in parables
and pronounce the next Aeon
as he announced the fleshly Aeon as Noah.

Regarding his words, he spoke in seventy-two tongues;
he opened heaven's doors and shamed Hell's tyrant!

He awakened the dead and destroyed Satan's power!

Then turmoil broke loose.
The Archons were enraged and wished to capture him
And hand him over as a prisoner to the tyrant of Hell.

They tempted one of his disciples
and set fire to the soul of one named Judas,
who delivered him to the temporal power.

They seized and tried him,
bringing down Justice upon themselves,
delivering him to Sasabeck, Governor of Hell,
for nine brazen shekels.

This Saviour prepared himself to descend and shame them,
but Sasabeck captured him.

But he discovered that this Saviour's true nature
couldn't be seized to hand over to the Archons.

"Who is this, what is this?" he enquired.
"He's destroyed the Aeonic law;
he's from the Logos of Life's Great Power.
He's triumphed over the Archonic rule
and they are powerless."

The Archons tried to find out what had happened.
They failed to see this was the beginning of their end
and the ancient Aeon would change.

The Sun eclipsed, all was darkness,
wicked spirits became fearful.
They saw he'd soon rise up and the signification
of the new Aeon would be proclaimed
and old Aeons would vanish.

Those who know these events will be blessed
and will unveil them, for they've known truth
and found heavenly peace.

Many will follow him and toil in their own lands;
they'll travel and become scribes,
writing down his teachings.

These Aeons have now vanished;
So, how vast was the Aeonic ocean that has gone?
What size are these Aeons?
How should mankind make ready for the new Aeon?
How will they become steady, deathless Aeons?

After teaching, the Saviour announced the second Aeon;
the first disappeared after he had preached for
one hundred and twenty years.

This is the ideal number that is highly revered;
he made the western fringe a wasteland
and destroyed the eastern edge.

This is written to inform your offspring
and all who wish to follow our Great Logos
and his declaration.

Then the Archons raged, as they burned,
shamed by their destruction.
They smouldered, waxing wrathfully at this life.

Their towns were shattered, their mountains quaked;
the vultures came and dined on their dead.

The earth lamented in grief with the people
and they despaired.

When these days were over, evil arose again
until the end of the Logos.

The Archons of west and east vowed
to perform the task of tempting men into sin.

They desired to annihilate true teaching
and words of wisdom while encouraging falsehood.

The Archons assailed the venerable teachings,
wishing to spread iniquity,
so they pretended to be worthy.

But they were impotent because the corruption
within them was too great.

Then the Great Logos became enraged
And wished to visit their land.

The time arrived, when he'd grown from a babe to manhood,
and the Archons sent a deceitful impersonator
to steal his knowledge of his Great Power.

They hoped to tempt him to perform miracles,
to reign over the world and lead mankind astray.

Then the impersonator would teach circumcision
and condemn the uncircumcised Gentiles,
who are a true people.

He sent many false teachers in advance of the time to come,
when he'll scour souls of purity and make evil more effective.

The oceans will dry up,
the heavens will cease sending morning dew,
the river springs will silt up,

the deep will be laid bare and wasted,
the stars made to wax large and the sun extinguished!

Then the Great Logos, the Christ,
will retreat with all who know him
and enter the infinite light,
where there's no one of lustful flesh to take them prisoner.

They will be free and holy; nothing will assail them.
He shall guard them as they wear sacred robes
which fire cannot burn, nor black night
or fierce storm cause their true vision to cease.

Then he'll vanquish the wicked;
they'll be punished and cleansed.
Their time of power will be confined
to fourteen hundred and sixty years.

When fire has destroyed all, it will consume itself.
The work will be fulfilled;
compassion and knowledge will thrive!

The heavens will fall into the deep,
the sons of materialism will die.
Souls will appear who have been made holy
through the light of the Great Power
which is above all powers, infinite, universal,

"I AM," and those who know me.

They'll dwell in the Aeon of Justice and Beauty
for they are prepared in truth,
having worshipped inscrutable unicity
and known Him through His will,
which is in them as their own.

And all will be as mirrors of His great light,
shining and finding rest in His peace.

He'll free the souls being punished
and they shall be purified.
All shall be purified.
They'll know the saints and pray
"Have compassion on us, Great Power,
who is superior to all other powers."

For in the tree of life, those that see evil
will be made blind; we'll not search for them
for they do not search for us or have faith in us.
But they acted because of the Archons and their Lords.

We have acted according to our birth in the creation
of the Archon of Great Power which brings Law,
and we're the immutable Aeon!

THE SOPHIA OF JESUS CHRIST

This complex revelational discourse given by the Resurrected Christ describes invisible celestial regions. Christ is the Incarnation of the Gnostic Saviour and Sophia the female personification of Divine Wisdom, an archetype of the Great Mother.

After his resurrection from the dead,
Christ's twelve disciples, with the seven women,
went to the Mountain of Divination and Joy at Galilee.

They were concerned about the substratum of the universe,
its plan, the power of the State, Divine providence,
and the Saviour's hidden way towards them.

When suddenly he appeared, not in his familiar form
but as an invisible, almost palpable, spirit.
His similitude resembled a vast angel of pure light.

I must not describe his plenitude;
no human mind could bear it, only pure souls.
It was that on which he'd preached, at the Mount of Olives.

He said, "My peace be with you, I hand it to you all."
They were amazed and quaked.

Jesus laughed and said, "Why are you so concerned.
What are you seeking?"

Philip answered, "We are questing for the knowledge
underlying substance and the Divine plan."

Jesus replied, "I wish you to understand
that all born into this world from its beginning until now,
being earthbound, although enquiring about God,
haven't yet found Him.

The wisest have pondered on the ordainment of the world
and its motion, but they haven't found the Truth.

Ordainment is controlled threefold,
claim philosophers, who can't agree.

Some think it's self-motivated,
that it's Divine providence or fate.

It's none of these! None are near the Truth
for they reason with man's limited mind.

But I my Self, who emanates from pure boundless Light.
I AM here, I know God.

I can tell you about the precise nature of Truth.

What emerges from itself is impure and self-generated;
providence lacks Wisdom and fate lacks discrimination.

It's given to you to understand,
and whoever's fit will understand!
Not those conceived through impure intercourse,
but He who's conceived by the Primal energy is eternal
in the midst of mankind."

Matthew said, "Master, nobody can find Truth
except through you, so pray tell us!"

Jesus answered, "He who is beyond words is inscrutable,
not subject to mastery, from the world's beginning until now.

Except for Himself alone and anyone else
He wishes to inform.

He who IS comes from primordial Light;
I am that unborn, deathless Saviour.

Since He isn't subject to any object, He is nameless;
He that is named is the notion of another.

He is formless but has a strange representation,
like no one else, superior even to the universal.

He sees all sides and knows His own Self,
from and by Himself, boundless, unknowable,
deathless, beyond comparison.
He is immutable goodness,
perfect, without flaw, immortal.

He knows His own Self beyond measure,
leaving no mark, pristine without blemish,
ever blessed, The Father of All."

Philip asked, "Master, how did He come to the Elect?"

Jesus replied, "Before anything can be seen
from what is visible, it must be known
that the sovereignty and glory are with Him.

He contains All, while nothing contains Him.
He is all Wisdom, reason, reflection and power.

All these forces are equal and form the source of All.

The whole of mankind from beginning to end
was known in his foresight,
for He is the boundless unborn Father of All."

Thomas asked, "Lord, how did these powers come to be
and why were they created?"

Jesus answered, "I come from the limitless
that I might inform you about the All.

The Spirit who had this power gave birth
and created nature's forms,
so the great prodigality concealed
in him might be revealed.

Because of his compassion and unconditional love,
he wished to bear such fruit so he need not enjoy
his abundant perfection alone.

Reason reveals how faith in unseen powers was found
in the seen and is owned by the Unborn Father.
Whoever has ears to hear, let him hear!

The Almighty King of the Universe
is called not just Father, but also our Grand Father,
for He was the source of all that was to come.

Seeing His own Self as if reflected in a mirror,
He manifested, representing Himself.

His similitude was the Divine Self, and Father;
the opponent of all that opposes.

Primordial, Unborn, Self-existent,
equal in eternity with His own Light,
but greater in power.

Then there appeared myriad self-generated souls,
equal in eternity and force, whose kind is named the
'Generation Without A Kingdom'.

These are they from whom you've come, named mankind.
Sons of the unborn Father whose similitude is within you.
Full of everlasting glory, unspeakable joy and infinite
celebration!
This wasn't realised before among all Aeons and their
worlds."

Matthew asked, "How was man brought into Being?"

The Perfect One replied, "He who always existed,
before the Universe was created entered into eternity,
as the Self Originated Father, full of effulgent light.

Then He willed His similitude to become an almighty power.
Instantly the essence of that pure light became immortal,
Androgyne Man.

So that through this immortality
man might attain Self Knowledge
and awaken from his deep sleep of forgetfulness.

Through the grace of the divine messenger,
who'll be with you 'til the end,
even midst this spiritual poverty of thieves.

His bride is the Magnificent Sophia, who first,
through immortal man, appeared as Divinity, the Kingdom
and the Father, the Self-originated, who revealed all.

He formed a great Aeon for his Sovereignty,
and as King reigned over the universe of spiritual poverty.

He created gods, archangels and innumerable angels
for his Kingdom of Light.

And the male triumvirate that was in Sophia
brought forth God, Divinity and the Kingdom.
He was Named God of Gods and King of Kings.

Archetypal man has a unique intellect,
powers of self-reflection, and reason.

His qualities are perfect and eternal
but his powers are unequal, like a son to his Father.

The monad, the simple unity, was primal in creation.
All that manifested was formed
and named by His Great Power.

The distinction between the born and the unborn was made.
Now Eternal Man is full of undying glory and holy joy;
his whole kingdom rejoices for ever."

Bartholomew asked, "Why was he called Son of Man.
Who is Father to this Son?"

The Saviour answered, "Primordial Archetypal Man
is creative, Self-perfected wisdom.

He meditated with his bride Sophia and his first offspring
was born, an androgyne.

His male part is named the Son of God.

His female part, the Sophia,
Mother of the Universe.

Her name is Love; the son is Christ
since he derived power from his Father,
who created angels from spirit and light."

His disciples said, "Lord, tell us about Man
so we may know his glory."

Jesus replied,
"Whoever has ears to hear, let him hear!

The first Procreator or father is Adam, eye of light,
for he came from radiant light with His holy angels,
beyond speech and without shadow.
Praising with great joy their powers of reflection,
inherited from their Father.

The whole Kingdom of the Son of Man,
the Son of God, is full of indescribable,
shadowless joy, constant celebration
and rejoicing at his undying glory,
never known before nor revealed in previous Aeons.

I came from that Primordial, Self-originated, primal,
boundless light, that I may tell you all."

His disciples asked once more,
"Tell us simply how they descended from the invisible,

the undying realms, to the world that dies."

The perfect saviour said,
"The Son of man agreed with Sophia, his consort.
He displayed a vast androgyne light;
his male name is Saviour of All.

His female name is All Procreator, Sophia Pistis.

All born into this world, descending like a ray
from His radiant light, are sent by the Almighty
to return eventually to Him, and be ever protected.

The bondage of man's ignorance tied him to Sophia's will
so that the whole world, in spiritual poverty,
could see its arrogance and blindness.

But I come from a realm above,
sent by the will of the Great Light
that escaped from this bondage.

I have stopped the pillage of thieves,
I have awakened that ray sent by Sophia
that my work might bear good fruit.

And through me men might be perfected
and not be defective, unified through me,

the Great Saviour, so God's glory might be revealed.

Sophia felt justified, and her sons determined
to achieve honour and glory and return to their Father
and understand the Word of masculine light.

You, my disciples, were called by me
that you might receive that Light
and free yourselves from the power of dark forces.

Then the world will no more manifest before you
because of unclean carnal intercourse
and the fearsome power that comes from lust.
You'll stamp upon all evil intent!"

Then Thomas asked, "Lord, how many Aeons
are there that rise above even the heavens?"

Jesus answered,
"I praise you since you enquire about the Aeons,
for your own source is in the limitless.

When what I've stated was revealed, The Self Originator,
the Father, created twelve Aeons as spheres
for His twelve angels.

All these were perfect and filled with goodness,
but a flaw in the female portion appeared.

The first Aeon is the Son of Man, the Primal Procreator,
the Saviour who is now come.
The second is Archetypal Man, Adam, eye of light.

That which contains these is that Aeon,
subject to no other kingdom, the everlasting boundless
Self-Originated Aeon of all Aeons.
The Aeon above the seventh came from Sophia,
the first Aeon.

Immortal man displayed his Aeons, powers and kingdoms,
granting rule to all who manifest in him.
So they might fulfil their will until the ending
of the last matter that hangs above chaos.

The Aeons agreed with one another
and displayed their greatness
from spirit with myriad brilliant lights.

In the genesis they were given names:
the first Aeon, the beginning; the second, the intermediate,
and the third, the perfect.

The first was termed Unification and Peace.

The third was called 'Congregation',
from the vast multitude that appeared
in the multitudinous.

So when the multitude congregates,
they come to the unification termed Congregation,
from that same name, which exceeds heaven.

The Congregation of the eighth Aeon was androgyne,
part male, part female.

The male was termed Congregation;
the female, Life, so it might be shown that from
the female issued Life, in all Aeons.
Each name was accepted from the beginning!

Gods created from their contemplation,
lords, archangels and angels.
Similitudes emerged with substance, shape and name,
for all Aeons and worlds.

The immortals derive their power from Immortal Man,
who is named Silence.

He, by ruminating without words,
established his own sovereignty.

The Deathless Ones created a great kingdom
in the eighth sphere.
With temples, thrones and heavens for their own Kings.

All this happened by the will of the Divine
Universal Mother."

Then the Apostles said, "Lord, pray tell us about
those who live in the Aeons."

The Saviour replied, "Hosts of angels, virgin spirits
and radiant lights were created for their might and splendour.

They are free from illness and frailty.
So all Aeons and heavens,
in the splendour of Immortal Man
and Sophia, were created.

All subsequent creation followed this archetypal image,
in the heavens of chaos and their dependent worlds.

All natures emerging from primordial chaos
are in shadowless light, unspeakable joy
and unutterable celebration.

They are glorified in absolute peace
among all Aeons and powers.

All that I've said is to aid you shine in light
even more than these!"

Mary asked,
"Lord, from where did your disciples come?
Where are they going? What should they do?"

Jesus answered, "Sophia the Mother,
and her husband, wished to create all
without male intervention.

But by the will of the Father of All,
that His infinite Love might be made known,
He wove a veil between the Immortals and all
that followed.

Each Aeon and chaos risks that female imperfection
might occur and errors may oppose her will.

These became the veil of spirit from Aeons
above the Light.

A ray descended to God's nether regions in chaos,
so their shapes might come from that beam;
it's a judgement on the Arch-Procreator,
called Yaldabaoth.

That ray revealed their sculpted shapes
through His breath, as living souls.

This spirit fell fast asleep in the soul's ignorance.

Then it was warmed from the breath of the male light
And attained the power of Reason.

Names were given to all in chaos;
this happened by the will of Sophia,
that Immortal Man might weave
special ropes, as justice for thieves.

He welcomed the breath but, as a soul, he wasn't fit
to seize that power until chaos was completed,
as ordained by the Archangel.

I've taught you all about Immortal Man and
released the ropes of thieves from his power.

I've shattered the doors of the merciless ones
and subdued their evil intent until they're ashamed
and struggle upwards from dark ignorance.

That's why I've come! So spirit and breath
might be united and two become one.

From the first, ripe fruit grows and rises up to Him
who is from the genesis, in unspeakable joy and splendour.

All shall honour our Father's Grace;
whoever knows about the Supreme God who reigns
above the whole universe shall stamp on their own death,
frustrate their evil inclination, cut the knot of their ignorance,
awaken my grace and aid, and trample over dark powers!"

These are the words spoken by the Perfect Saviour,
Lord Jesus Christ.

He left his disciples everlastingly in their spirit's holy joy,
and they went to teach his living Gospel of God,
the everlasting unborn spirit.

Amen

HUMAN SUFFERING

A fragment by the famed Gnostic, Basilides of Alexandria (second century AD), who believed that the Will of God is Omnipotent and Good, and that Suffering is a form of Divine Justice and has a reformative value. He wrote many important Gnostic commentaries on the Gospels.

Basilides said, "I have faith that all who suffer
have missed the mark more than they know,
in this or another life, and now shall come to
a beneficial end."

Paul told the Romans,
"Once, I lived separated from the law."

He meant that before this life he lived in a body
not subjected to God's law.

By the Divine grace which directs them,
they may be reviled for irrelevant crimes
and not be compelled to suffer as convicted criminals,
adulterers or murderers.

But instead they endure trials because they are Christians,
which ameliorates their pain.

But even if an egotism suffers without sin,
which is most unusual, the torment isn't forced
by the conspiracy of some authority.

It's more like the wails of a newborn babe,
who seems to be innocent.

THE GOSPEL
OF TRUTH

T his powerful early Greek Gnostic Treatise covers topics such as "The Quest for the Father", the "Hope of Salvation" and the "Need for a Saviour". All will help to redeem the Soul from its ignorance.

The Gospel of Truth is sheer perfection and holy joy!

For all those who've received their Father's grace
by knowing who He really IS.

Through the force of His Word,
which issued from the fullness of the Godhead.

That is Christ, who is in the heart of his Father,
with the sacred task he's been set,
to save and enlighten those in ignorance.
This gospel gives hope of certainty
for all who diligently enquire.

When the Whole went seeking for the One

from whom All come, the All was found to
be the Divine Self, Almighty God,
inscrutable, indescribable, supreme.

Nescience had caused anxiety and fear,
a smutty fog that made people feel blind.

Error became potent and, through folly,
began creating with force and beauty a falsity of truth.

This wasn't an embarrassment for the inscrutable,
indescribable Supreme; it was as nothing,
this angst, forgetfulness and guile,
for Real Truth is unchanging perfection.

From this fact, learn to hate error,
which lacked knowledge of the source
and dropped into dense mist, regarding the Father,
forming illusion to frighten and seize those beings
existing in the intermediate realm.

The Father didn't cause this error,
although all emanates from Him.

Knowledge came from Him,
that forgetfulness which causes error
might be destroyed.

The Gospel of Christ, when sought,
reveals the secret mysteries
to those purified through His grace,
enlightening all encased in darkness through forgetfulness.

He pointed out the Way of Truth, which he preached.
Error became enraged, persecuted and attacked him,
but was nullified by his sacrifice.

Crucified, he became a source of Knowledge
concerning his Father.

It didn't lead to annihilation because his Way was practised.
Those who practised rejoiced, discovering Him in themselves.

As for the inscrutable, unknowable One, the Father,
the Flawless One, who created the All
and contains the All and whom the All always needs,
He held flawlessness within himself,
which He didn't pass on to the All; He wasn't envious;
what envy could there possibly be
between Himself and the All?

For if the Age had received His flawlessness,
the All wouldn't have returned to the Father.

He holds their flawlessness, granting it as a boon
to those who return to Him
with perfect knowledge of the Unity.

It is He who created the All; in Him dwells the All;
All have great need of Him.

Our Father wills that the nescient
will eventually know and love Him.

Christ was teacher of All, peaceful and at ease.
In houses of devotion he came and spoke His Word.

Philosophers, wise in their own opinion, tried to refute Him.
He defeated them for they were ignorant,
and in their folly they came to hate him.

Children came, those to whom knowledge of their Father
hadn't been forgotten, and he strengthened them.

They learned about, they knew, they worshipped the Father.
The living gospel of the Father
was inscribed on their hearts' splendour!
That which pre-existed in the Father's will
before His creation,
within His inscrutability.

That secret tome which nobody could steal,
for anyone who stole it would perish.

Nobody among the faithful would have been saved
unless this tome had been revealed.

The all-loving Christ was long-suffering
in bearing the suffering of others,
until he received that tome, since he knew his own death
would bring new life for the multitude.

When a rich householder dies there's often a secret clause
in his will revealing his fortune.

So it was with the All which dwelled secretly,
while our Father of the All,
from whom all space emanated, remained unseen.

When Christ came, he became the Gnosis
of that secret tome and was crucified.

He revealed the tome of his Father by his death on the cross.
Such a magnificent teaching!

He attracts his own death,
although Life Everlasting is his robe of glory.

Having thrown off transient tatters,
he donned the cloak of durability, which nobody could steal.
Having come to the vale of fear, he walked through it.

Those who were naked and unclothed through forgetfulness
gained understanding and flawlessness.
Then they taught the truth from their hearts,
to those open to receive.

Those who were willing to learn his doctrine are alive
and are inscribed in the book of life.

It is about their own Real Self that they hear teaching,
receiving it from their Father
and turning inwards towards Him.

It is necessary that the All shall aspire towards Him,
for the flawlessness of the All is in Him.

If the aspirant has understanding,
the Father takes him back to Himself.
For he who is trapped in nescience lacks,
and what he lacks is crucial.

He needs that Self Knowledge which will make him flawless.
For the flawlessness of the All dwells in the Father;
they must turn inwards towards Him.

He chose them beforehand
and matured those who came from Him.
Those whose names He knew in advance
were summoned for the end.

Thus the names the Father has uttered have understanding;
the names of the uncalled remain nescient.

Those who stay in nescience until the end
are people of forgetfulness and will vanish.
Why are these wretched ones nameless and not summoned?

Only he who has the understanding
that descends through grace is called.
He listens, responds, turns within and cleaves towards Him.
He acknowledges His call
and yearns to perform his Father's will;
he wishes to please Him and is rewarded with peace.

Each name comes before Him,
knowing from where he came and where he is going.

The Chosen knows, like a drunkard
who has returned to sobriety.
Christ has rescued many from falsehood;
he has visited their hearts, from which they had strayed.

Because of an abyss they fell into falsehood,
the void which encloses a space in which nothing is enclosed.

It was a miracle: they were within the Father
while not recognising Him,
and they were able to walk on,
for they failed to understand
or to know the One in whom they dwelled.

If His will hadn't issued from Him as revelation,
the knowledge of how His various rays harmonise
would have stayed in nescience.

This is the Knowledge of the Book of Life
He gave to twenty-three Aeons at the end.

He showed how His sacred letters
are neither vowels nor consonants,
so that one could read them
and think they were unwise.
Yet they are letters of Truth
to those who know how to read.

Each letter is a total conception, like a whole volume,
for they are letters inscribed by the One!

Our Father composed them for all Aeons
so they would know Him.

His wisdom meditates on His Word,
His doctrine unveils His knowledge.

Patience is its crown; joy is in perfect concord.
His splendour uplifts that which His will has unveiled.

His peace has taken it into itself, His love has enrobed it,
His faithfulness has taken it to heart.

In this way the Word of Almighty God the Father
advances into the All,
as the fruit of His heart's core and the seal of His will.

It maintains the All, elects them and absorbs its effect.
It purifies, leading them back to Him
and into the Divine Mother,
also to the Christ of infinite sublimity.

The Father unveils His heart, the Holy Spirit.
He reveals what is secret, His son,
so through His grace the aeons may know Him
and cease toiling in seeking Him,
but abide in Him, knowing that is true peace.

Having remedied the lack He destroyed the form,
the sphere in which He worked.

For where there's jealousy and conflict, it's lacking;
but where there's Oneness, there lies flawlessness.

The lack manifests because our Father was unknown;
when He's known, that will vanish.

It's like a man in nescience;
when knowledge comes, nescience is dissolved.

Night disappears when dawn breaks;
lack dissolves in the flawlessness.

From that time on, form is invisible
and disappears in mingling with the One.

Now its works lie fragmented in time;
Oneness will become flawless
and in time make all space the same.

He creates whomever and whatever;
He wills by bestowing name and form
and causes those that are born
to be unaware of their Creator.

Those yet to be born are as nothing, but are in Him
and wish to be born when He wills;
like in the time to come.

Before all manifests, He knows what He'll create and destroy.
But His unborn fruit are ignorant
and can do nothing without His grace.

All space in our Father is from the One,
who created it from nonexistence.

He who has no root has no shoot,
and although he imagines he has come into existence,
he will cease.
For he who doesn't truly exist
can never come into fullness of flawless Being.

How then did he regard himself?
As one who comes into existence
like night-time shadows and ghosts.
But when the Light shines on his fright
he sees that he is as nothing.

So they were in ignorance of their Father,
He being invisible to them.
Since through fear, turmoil, imbalance,
doubt and strife, there were myriad delusions.

Imaginary souls lost in heavy torpor,
full of agonising dreams.

Either they're trying to escape without help
or they come hunting after others.
Striking blows or receiving them,
falling from heights or flying in air.
Being slain without a slayer or slaying their friends,
covered in blood.

When those that suffer these nightmares wake up,
they see them as nothing for they themselves are nothing.

Such is the path of those who've shed their nescience,
like a dream without substance.
The knowledge of their Father
comes as something of great worth,
like a glorious sunrise.

Each one lived as if in a deep sleep when ignorant,
and awoke on realisation of the Good
when he returned to the Father.

Blessed is he who restores the sight of the spiritually blind!
The Holy Spirit chased them with great haste,
to wake them up!

Holding out his hand to those lying helpless on the earth,
he pulled up those that were not yet awakened!
He told them how to know their Father and His Son.

When they'd seen and heard Jesus,
he showed them how to savour and feel him,
the beloved one.

When Christ came teaching about their Father,
the unknowable, inscrutable one,
he breathed into them meaning, action and will,
revealing the Light to very many.
Instantly they turned inwards towards him.

The materialists were exiles
and failed to see his similitude,
and couldn't know him.
He came in bodily form without obstacles,
for purity is unconquerable.

He again revealed new doctrine
about what's in our Father's heart,
having revealed His perfect Word!

When the Light had shone,
through his lips as well as his voice,
all Life was given new birth.

He passed on to them his apperception of comprehension,
compassion and redemption.

Energy of spirit flowed from our Father's
boundlessness and sublimity,
ending chastisement and torment,
for some had been led astray
from the light of His countenance.

Those in need of mercy had fallen into falsehood and bondage.
He vanquished these foes by his strength
and enlightened them with his teaching.

He became the Way for sheep who had strayed
from knowledge into nescience.
He was a great find for seekers,
a foundation for those toppling,
flawlessness for those corrupted.

He was the good shepherd
who deserted the ninety-nine that were safe
and searched for that one that had strayed.
He celebrated when he found the lost sheep,
for ninety-nine is a number held in the left hand.

When one more is found,
one hundred is a number held by the right.

It attracts what was lacking in the left
and places it in the right.

One hundred signifies soundness;
it is our Father's number.

Even on the Sabbath day he laboured
for the sheep fallen into the ditch.
He breathed new life into them
so they might know the Truth inwardly
and become sons of inner knowledge.

What kind of Sabbath is it that forbids salvation
to work so you may live?

From daylight above which knows no night,
and from that sun which never sets because it is flawless.
Utter from the heart "I am the perfect day!
And in me dwells that light which never sets."

Teach the Truth to those that seek,
and knowledge to those fallen into the pit through falsehood.
Steady the stance of all who've slipped
and reach out with open arms
to all those who are sick at heart.

Feed the famished, grant peace to the fatigued,
raise up all who wish to arise,
awaken all who wish to awaken!
For you are the comprehension
that has been brought forward into light.

If power acts, it becomes more powerful!

Pay attention to your own Real Self!
Don't spend time on that which you've rejected
from your petty self.
Don't return to the vomit you've thrown up.

Don't be like moths or worms that cause decay,
for you've already cast them out.
Don't make a home for Satan;
you've already vanquished that fiend!
Don't hold up those that form barriers
which have nearly fallen.

The lawless are the ones to scorch, rather than the just.
The lawless work alone;
the righteous work amongst their flock.

Do the will of our Father; we all come from Him!
Our Father is sublime; His will is beneficent.
He has watched over you so you may find peace.

He takes notice of your works
because His children are His incense,
the grace of His Face.

Our Father loves His fragrance and reveals it everywhere.
It combines with matter and bestows perfume
on His light and peace;
He makes it superior to shape and sound.

It's not the senses that smell the perfume but the breath,
which attracts His fragrance to itself and is subsumed.

He preserves and transfers it back to its original home,
from where it first emerged,
the primary fragrance that has grown cold.

It is a subtle form, like ice which once was liquid,
but when breathed on, heats up.
Cold fragrance comes from duality,
so faith comes and dissolves division!

And brings forward the intense heat
of the Godhead that lives in Christ,
the Pleroma of Love.

So frigidity will never return,
and there'll be Oneness and flawless thought.

This is the promise of the Pleroma,
for those who wait for salvation from above.
While the hope on which they are waiting
lies in the waiting.

For those whose similitude is light without shadow,
the Pleroma is on its way.
The lack isn't because of the boundlessness of our Father,
who allows time for the lack to be healed.

Although no one says,
"The Flawless One must come this way."

But the deepening of our Father's Love is extensive
and the concept of falsehood is nonexistent in Him.

It is faith which may fall
but can again stand up in the knowing of Him,
and he who has been chosen and who shall return;
this is metanoia.

So flawlessness breathed,
and chased away the sins of those who'd fallen,
to find repose.

Forgiveness is the light in the lack,
the Word of the Pleroma.

The doctor rushes to where the disease is rampant
because it is his will.

He who bears a lack does not conceal it
because someone possesses what the other lacks.

So the Pleroma, which is not lacking,
fills any lack in what it provides for itself to fulfil.
So we might receive grace,
for when we lacked, grace was deficient.

That causes our contraction to smallness in a graceless place.
When this contraction was received,
He unveiled that which was lacking, the Pleroma.
The finding of the Light of Truth,
which arose because it is constant.

This is why Jesus is referred to as being "in their midst".
So those in perplexity might receive a turning inwards,
and he might anoint them with his precious salve.
The salve is our Father's infinite compassion
and unconditional love, which He hands to them.

Those whom He's anointed have become flawless;
full jars receive ointment.
The jar empties of ointment because there was a lack,
and the salve was applied.

His breath attracts healing, by its own power;
for those without lack, no seal need be broken nor salve used.
What they lack our flawless Father refills.

He is good; He knows his plants,
because it is He who planted them in His own garden.

Now His Eden is a haven of peace.
This is the flawlessness in the will of our Father
and these are the words of His contemplation.

Each one of His words comes from His will,
in the unveiling of His Word.

While they were at peace
through the depth of His meditation,
which was the First,
there issued a mind that spoke
the one Word of silent grace.
This was termed "thought",
for they were held in it before it was unveiled.

It was the First, when the will of Him who willed,
so willed it.
His will is what our Father lives in, and is satisfied.
Nothing ever happens without Him,

nor can anything happen without His will,
which is inscrutable.

His mark is the will that no one can know Him.

Nor is it possible to investigate Him so as to know Him.

What He wills is "that",
even if it displeases those in the way,
seeking God, desiring our Father.

For He knows all their beginnings and their ends.
At their end He'll enquire of them, directly.

The end is the final receipt of knowledge about He
who is concealed and is our Father.
From whom the genesis issued and to whom all shall return.

They have issued from the splendour
and rejoicing of His Holy Name.

The name of our Father is the Son.
It is He who first named the One
who came from Him and is Himself.

He is that One to whom belongs all that exists around Him,
and that is our Father.

His is the Name; His is the Son;
He can be known.

The Name is unseen because it is the enigma of the unseen,
which comes to ears that are full of Him.

Our Father's name is unutterable,
but known through His Son.

The Name is Great.
Who will be capable of uttering His holy Name?

Only our Father, who owns the Name,
and his sons, in whom the Name lives.

Since our Father is unborn,
He alone is the One who created for Himself the Name,
before He created the Aeons,
so that His Name as Father might rule as Lord.

That is His Name in Truth,
stable in control, through His flawless force.

His Name is wordless.
Nor does His Name consist of mere names; it is unseen.

He gave the Name to Himself alone,

for only He can know Himself
and has the power to give a Name.

For the nonexistent is nameless,
but the One who exists lives with a name
and He alone knows it.

The Father, the Son, is His Name!

He never concealed it in matter, but it lived as for the Son;
He alone gives a Name.
The Name is Father, for that Name is also the Son.

Where indeed would Divine mercy find a Name
except in our Father?

A man will ask his neighbour,
"Who is it who can give a Name to Him
who existed before Himself?"
As if children never received a name from their parents.

First we must pursue the enquiry,
"What does the Name mean?"

It is the Name in Truth,
not the Name from our Father but the Real Name!
He didn't receive the Name on credit, as others might,

according to the way that each name is given.

But this is the Real Name;
there's no one there to give it to Him,
for He's unnameable, inscrutable, unknowable.

Until that time when He who is flawless
speaks of Him alone,
it is He who has authority to utter the Name and know it.

When it pleased Him that His Name, which is beloved,
should be His Son, He named him
"He who came from the deep".

Christ spoke about concealed secrets,
knowing our Father is the Supreme Being
without wickedness.

So he brought himself to teach about
where He came from and where He rests.
And to preach about the splendour of the Pleroma,
the magnitude of his Father and His Divine sublimity.
About the place from where he came
and the realm where he was confirmed.

He'll be quick to return, receiving manna and growth,
and his dwelling in the Pleroma.

All the rays from our Father are Pleromas,
and the source is the One who created them in His own Self.
He designated their fate; each is created
so through their own will they may return.

For where they place their will, their source,
He lifts them to the great spiritual heights of their Father.

They rest their burden on His head and they're maintained,
welcoming Him as if they'd greeted His face with kisses.

Yet they don't always act this way for they are not so exalted,
yet they are not deficient in their Father's splendour.

They didn't regard their Father as diminutive or severe,
or liable to anger, but knew that He was without evil,
unshakeable and sublime, knowing all space before
they originated and without need to be taught.

This is the way of those who already have some taste
from above of His boundless magnitude.

As they attend on the flawless One
who waits for them with open arms,
they won't descend to hell,
nor suffer envy, pain and death.

They will rest in peace, neither toiling
nor being twisted around the Truth.
For they are Truth; their Father is within,
they are in Him, who is flawless!
Undivided in His beneficence, lacking nothing,
at perfect peace, rejuvenated in Spirit.

They'll be attentive to finding their own source
and not endure loss to their soul.
This is the isle of the blessed, this is their golden land.

The rest must understand that it's inappropriate for me,
being in His place, to speak about anything else.

It is from there that I come to be
and it is right to attend all the time
to our Father of All and our real brothers,
those who benefit from His unconditional love,
which is constantly poured out,
for He dwells in their midst.

They demonstrate in Truth
and dwell in Life Everlasting
and witness His Flawless Light
filled with their father's seed,
which lives in His heart and the Pleroma,
while His Holy Spirit celebrates

and magnifies the One in whom He lives.

He is goodness;
His offspring are flawless,
fit to bear His Name.

He is our Father;
we are His children whom He loves!

THE GREATEST HUMAN EVIL IS FORGETFULNESS OF GOD

A n early Gnostic text warning of the grave spiritual dangers
should the Soul lose hold of its essential Self. It stresses the
need for Recollection and Self Remembering leading to
eventual salvation.

FROM CORPUS HERMETICUM VII

Dear fellows, where are you rushing to like drunkards,
tipsy and staggering on the rich wine of reason,
forgetful of God?

You cannot stomach it; already you're about to vomit!

Halt! Sober up!
Elevate yourself by mental power.
Maybe not all of you can do that, but some of you can!

For the degeneration that flows from forgetfulness
is drowning the earth, infecting soul and body,
veiling the soul like a cloak
and stopping you from abiding in the heart.

So don't be swept away by this mad flood!

Find the way into your heart!
Look for a good teacher to show you the path
to the gates of remembrance.
Where there's a light, radiant and bright,
free from darkness.

Where nobody is drunk, but keeps their mental eye
on that Great Being who wills to be known in their heart.
That Great Being cannot be seen or heard,
or spoken or thought about, only by a higher subtle intellect
that transcends normal matters of the mind.

But first strip off the soiled cloak you wear,
the foul mantle of forgetfulness, the base of wickedness,
the link with evil, the black pit, the spiritual death,
the walking corpse, the moving coffin,
the domestic rogue who feeds on guile,
which he relishes, and conspires to cause your downfall.

Such is the habit; the filthy coat you've put on,
that is your foe!
It suffocates you and drags you down to its cruel self,
into the gutter.

Otherwise, through aspiration and seeing the beauty of Truth
and the Good that dwells in you,
you will come to despise this vile enemy
who plots to destroy you.

It ruins the mind and pollutes the senses
by muddying them with gross materialism,
filling them with disgusting lust for inane pleasure,
to prevent you from understanding
what you should understand!

And, what is worse,
it will stop you from seeing forever
what you should really see!

THE SECRET BOOK ACCORDING TO ST JOHN I, II & III

*I*ntroductory extracts from the "Apocryphon of John", son of Zebedee, outlining Gnostic mythology. They see Almighty God as the Source of all Being and describe the structure of the Divine Cosmology before Genesis. Probably composed around AD 180.

One day John, brother of James, a son of Zebedee,
was going to synagogue.

A Pharisee called Arimanios met him and said,
"Where is your teacher, the one you followed?"

John replied, "He's gone back to the place he came from."
Arimanios said, "That Nazarene has confused you.
He lied and closed your mind
and put you off the teachings of our fathers!"

When I heard this I left the synagogue
and went into the desert.

I was upset and said to myself,
"How was our Saviour chosen?
Why did he enter this world, and who sent him?
And what is that place that we'll all go to?"

While I was musing, suddenly the heavens opened!
All creation glowed with light.

I was very frightened,
when I saw in the brilliant light a boy,
standing upright.

Then he changed into an old person,
then a young one, all in bright light,
so that there appeared, as it were, three beings in one form.

Then this multiformed image addressed me and said,
"John, why do you doubt? Why are you terrified?
Are you a stranger to visions?
Don't be frightened. It is I who am with you forever,
It is I who am the Father, Mother and Son.

I am uncorrupted and pure.
I've come to enlighten you on what exists,
what is to come, and what is to be.
So you may know about the spiritual and the material realm,
the invisible and the visible, and all about the Perfect Man.

Pay attention so you can pass this on to others like you,
from the inheritance of this Perfect Man,
so they might know Truth.

This is my book on the teachings of Jesus, my Messiah,
and the unveiling of God's mysteries, which he taught,
and his great teachings secreted in silence."

I asked this triadic figure if I might hear this Truth.

He proclaimed and answered:
"There is nothing that can rule over the One.
It is that One which is God and Father of the All.

The transcendent, immanent, deathless Self,
shining as pure light, which nobody can see.

This absolute spirit is more than a God,
for nothing is above Him and all is in Him.
He rests alone and is independent.
He is perfect; He needs nothing and lacks for nothing.

He is boundless, unsearchable,
immeasurable, invisible.
External, internal, eternal,
ineffable, unnameable.

He is flawless, impeccable, incorporeal;
neither great nor small.

He has no quantity, quality or attributes.
He is inscrutable and beyond time.

He is King of Kings, bestowing life,
knowledge, goodness, mercy and salvation.

He is at rest, in silence,
as primordial Being and pure Light.

He looks at himself alone in perfect peace,
the fount of living waters exercising divine will.

This complete totality, the Aeon above Aeons,
the power and glory, the virgin spirit,
the womb for creation, Mother-father,
archetypal Man, macrocosm and microcosm.

He gazed at the Whole,
in the pure light of Absolute Consciousness,
and conceived its sole offspring, a luminous spark.

He was granted a cooperative spirit,
which was clairvoyant intellect.

That spirit rested with the anointed one, the Christ,
and wished to create by the Word, from its Will.

By the grace of the spirit,
out of the light of the anointed,
all powers originated.

Beauty, as the first angel, Harmozel,
and with this eternal realm, loveliness, truth and form.

Oroiael is the second, angelic light,
reflection, cognisance and memory,

Daueithal was third, intelligence, love
and archetypal ideal form.

Eleleth was fourth,
perfection, peace and wisdom.

From his will the first manifestation was named:
the Primordial Man, the Adam.

His son Seth was placed in the second realm,
with the souls of Saints.

In the fourth realm were placed unrepentant souls,
unacquainted with the Perfection.

They later repented and inhabited the fourth light,
to glorify the invisible spirit.

Wisdom conceived an idea derived from herself,
to show an image.
But her consort did not agree,
so she conceived alone.

Her birth was imperfect for it lacked her consort's will
and had a misshapen form; it was named Ialtabaoth.

It was snake-like, with a leonine face,
and from its eyes flashed lightning.

She cast it out so none of the immortals might know it,
and enveloped it in a glowing cloud.

She put a throne in the middle of the cloud
so it would be invisible,
except to the Mother Of All Living.

Then the Primal Creator, Almighty God,
ordered all things in Perfection."*

*The two final verses commence a new development of ideas and are
omitted.

THUNDER

A unique Gnostic revelation by a mysterious Female Deity, stressing the importance of the essential "I Am-ness". Also known as the "Perfect Mind", it contains parallels with ancient Indian literature which refers to the I AM form.

I have issued from a Great Power
and visit all who contemplate me;
I have been discovered by those
who search diligently.

Pay attention, those that meditate upon me,
and listen well!
All of you who are patiently waiting,
take me to your Self!

Don't dismiss me from your mind
and don't let your inner voices despise me;
don't forget me at any time or place; be watchful!

I am the first and the last,
I am both respected and ignored,
I am both harlot and holy.

I am wife and virgin, mother and daughter,
organs of my mother, barren, yet many are my sons.

I am She whose marriage is auspicious,
but I am husbandless.

I am the midwife who doesn't carry the balm of birth pains.
I am bride and groom sired by my spouse;
I am mother of my father,
sister of my husband, and he's my son.

I am slave of He who anointed me.
I am ruler of my children,
But He is the One from whom I was born.
He shall be my Son in time; my strength is from Him!
I am the rod of His potency in His youthful virility,
and He is the staff of my old age.
Whatever He wills, happens.

I am the unfathomable silence
and the thought that comes often,
the voice of many sounds,
and the word that appears frequently.

I am the meaning of my Name.
Why am I despised?
Do you love me and hate those who love me too?

If you deny me then admit me,
You, who pretend to tell the truth about me, really lie.

Yet you who've lied about me also tell the Truth.
If you know me, forget me,
and those who don't know me, let them know!

I am knowledge and ignorance.
I am embarrassment and effrontery,
shameless and ashamed.
I am courage and fright.

I am war and peace. Listen!
I am disgraced yet almighty.

Notice my poverty and richness.
Don't be unkind to me when I'm
thrown out upon the ground.

You'll find me hidden in those yet to come;
don't peer at me when I'm on the dung heap.

Don't desert me or cast me out;
you'll find me in the Kingdom.

Don't gaze at me when I'm ejected
in disgrace, nor mock me.

Don't hurl me amongst those who are slain violently.
I am merciful and cruel.
Be vigilant!
Don't despise my servitude.
Don't admire my self-control;
don't forsake me in my ineptitude.

Never fear my power; don't hate my timidity
or pour scorn on my arrogance.

I am She who dwells in all terror,
the strength and the trembling.

I am She who is pathetic and pleased in a pleasant place.
I am stupid and I am wise.

Why do you despise me in your councils?
I'll be quiet among the quiet.

I shall manifest and speak, yet why do Greeks hate me?
I am a Philistine among Philistines,
yet have the wisdom of Athens
and craftiness of the barbarians.
My image is great in ancient Egypt,
but is nothing amongst Philistines.

I've been hated everywhere, but also adored.
I am that which people call life and you call death.

I am called the Law and lawlessness.
I am the hunted and the captured.

I am the dispersed and the collected.
I don't keep festivals, but have many feasts.

I am both godless and She who knows God is Great!
I am the One you've contemplated and mocked.

I am ignorant, yet I teach.
I am despised, yet admired.
I am the One who conceals and then reveals her Self.
But when you conceal your Self, I shall appear.

When you appear I'll hide.
Hold me to your Self from comprehension and regret.

Take me to your Self in ugly and ruined places.
Rob those who are good, even in their ugliness.

Ashamed, take me to your Self shamelessly;
scold my organs in yourself.

Advance, all that know me and my organs;
establish high creatures amongst the lowly.

March onto childhood;
don't hate that state because it appears tiny.
Don't reject greatness in smallness.

My nature is peace, but war comes from me.

I am an exile and a subject;
I am substance and unsubstantial.

Those who do not cling to me are ignoramuses,
but those who dwell in my substance know me.

Those who are close don't know me.
When you are near, I'm distant.
On the day you're distant, I am close.
I am within, in your heart;
I am your true nature,
the creativity of your Self.

THE COSMIC DRAMA

An important and detailed, somewhat philosophic, exposition, sometimes called the "Tripartite Tractate". This lengthy text comprehensively covers the revised Valentinian theological view of the world and the Gnostic myth of the cosmos and its creation. Most of the Gnostic concepts, including the Logos, are elaborately explained. The writer is unknown, but Heracleon has been suggested as a possible author. The work dates from the first half of the third century AD.

OUR FATHER

As far as we can expound on higher matters,
it is appropriate to start with Our Father,
the source of the whole,
from whom we've received the grace to compose this book.

Our Father exists primordially,
prior to anything else whatsoever,
material or spiritual, came into being or manifestation;
He is the unique, Self-originated, single One,
like the number 1,
for He is the first One and the only One
who can be called uniquely Himself, alone!

Yet He is not an isolated Being,
or else he couldn't possibly be called Our Father.

As His Name, Our Father, naturally implies, an offspring,
such as a son or daughter, but He, is the One,
like a tap root of a great oak tree, with many fruitful branches;
He is a Father in the real sense of the word,
as he can't be imitated and He is unchanging!
He is in truth, God Almighty,
there is no other God beside Him, nor is anyone His Father.

He is unborn and created the Whole, the "All",
and His Being is everlasting and infinite!
He is deathless, as He was never conceived,
but He lives eternally in conscious existence,
as "I Am that I Am", which is His foundation,
and "That" by which He is truly magnified,
He will never move Himself from that which He essentially Is,
nor can any other being cause Him to create anything
He has not Himself willed into existence!

He is inscrutable! immutable, formless,
and can never be, in any way, diminished!
His wisdom is beyond any mental conception,
His force is unfathomable,
He is all loving and full of blissful delight;
He alone is perfect Goodness,

full of righteousness and every virtue of worth,
free from malice.

Whoever possesses anything, it is due to Him,
because He gives tirelessly,
as He is munificent and full of compassion,
loving kindness, and mercy, which endures forever;
there is no place where He Is or Is Not,
from which he has issued, or into which he will end,
nor has He a prior form or model,
nor is there any hindrance or obstacle to hamper His will.

Nor is there any primal matter from which he creates, alone;
He is flawlessly complete, being perfect, the "All";
there are no Names adequate to describe Him,
no matter how splendid and glorious they be;
it is impossible for the mind to conceive Him,
or speech to describe Him;
His magnificence is unknowable
and his unfathomable depths are beyond all bounds.

This is the nature of the Unborn One, invisible and ineffable;
He alone is the only One who knows Himself as He truly is!
He transcends all wisdom, intellect, glory, beauty and bliss;
His power is in His Will, He rests in great silence,
He is infinite, unconditional Love.

As absolute consciousness-awareness
He is the Self of all Beings,
One without a second.

THE SON AND HIS CHURCH

He has a Son, who subsists in Him, exists in Him,
and endures forever and forever.
Just as the Father lives, so does His Son,
the one, begotten after Him, there is no other;
he is the first born, only Son,
who has his unknowable attributes of unsurpassing greatness,
sweet nature, with miraculous powers
that shower his abundant loving kindness on all.

Not only did the Son come into Being from the Genesis,
but so did his Church;
he who believes the Son is an only son,
is contrary to the birth of the Church;
this question is mysterious and enigmatic,
for as the Father is One,
and has shown Himself to Himself alone,
so too the Son is a brother to himself alone, as he is unborn!

He enquires into himself, with his Father's aid,
and bestows on his own true Self, honour, splendour and love!

and conceives himself to be His Son,
birthless and deathless ad infinitum;
so the question is resolved,
his offshoots being myriad, infinite, and indivisible;
all those who exist have issued from the Father
and His Son like kisses!

Just as many kiss one another with good will,
the kiss being single,
although it is one of very many kisses,
so the Church, consisting of many men and women,
like kisses, pre-existed the aeons,
that is the "aeons of the aeons";
this is the condition of these holy undying spirits
on which the Son essentially rests,
as a Father essentially rests on His Son.

AEONIC EMISSIONS

The Church lives in the adjuncts and attributes
in which the Father and Son live,
and subsists in the begetting of a multitude of aeons;
in a mysterious way they bestow, through these qualities,
the virtues through which the Church survives;
these include fellowship which they form, one with another,
and towards the Son for whose Name, and splendour, they live.

It is impossible for the mind to comprehend the Son's glory,
he is the flawlessness of that realm,
he is beyond words and names;
men and women only have the capacity to name themselves
and to apperceive their own true Selves,
as hitherto they haven't been well grounded in that power.

Those with Self Knowledge enjoy the jubilation of the unborn,
nameless, inscrutable, formlessness;
it is the perfection of Fatherhood,
so His overflowing love creates the birth of the aeons;
they were ever in His Will, when their Being was actualised.

The "Primal" wished to propagate
that which was lacking in comprehension,
so He begot aeons, like Himself;
since He is as He is, He is a source undiminished
by His own flow of perennial fresh water
and unconditional love;
while held in the Divine Will, in His concealed profundity,
the "profound" knew them,
but they weren't able to know the profundity
that they actually were!

They existed in the Father and didn't exist for themselves,
nor was it possible for them to know their own Selves
nor anything else! like seeds or a fetus.

Like His Word, he created them spermatically,
and those he was to generate, were not yet in Being;
their father primally willed them
so they might Be for Him and their own Selves
and in His Will as a subtle intelligent substance,
sown like a spermatic seed;
so they might realise He graciously granted them "form"
so they might know their Father as their own Self.

He named them "Father"
announcing all that exists through that Name
which they own, by virtue of the knowledge,
that they entered into Self existence,
because the glory which escaped their attention,
lay hidden in that Name!

The babe while in the womb feeds itself
before it knows its own mother,
so they had the one sacred work of seeking for Him,
knowing He lives, but yearning to find out who he truly Is?

The flawless Father is perfectly good,
he didn't bear them so they would only live as His idea,
but that they might also enter into His actual Being;
so He bestowed His Grace for them to know their own Selves,
that lives everlastingly; just as babes are born in daylight so
they might know their parents.

The Father creates the "All", first as a young child,
a drop from a spring, a bud from a vine,
a blossom from a branch,
all in need of nourishment for growth.

He witholds knowledge for a while;
He conceived and possessed it from the genesis,
knew it, but shut it off at first; not from envy,
but that these aeons might not receive their perfection
at the beginning
and raise themselves to their Father's Splendour
believing that they themselves achieved that feat
by their own greatness.

This was His grace; for the One from whom they learned,
the Son, who is full, whole, and perfect,
educated them with his own qaulities;
partaking of the Whole, in accordance with his law
that nobody can Know Himself by himself unaided.

The Father expanded space
and formed a firm foundation for the whole Universe,
and all that happens in it;
having planted Himself in their souls
that they might search for Him;
the joy of their quest consists in the knowledge that He exists,
and enquiring who it is that is existing?

This seeking nourishes the soul,
and through grace and effort, receives from Him,
illuminating through his fellow working,
granting knowledge, and mingling with thoughts that arise.

This is from the Son, the one whom they know
that it is he who robes their soul;
He comes from his Father who is beyond speech,
and conception, the first in Being;
He named Himself for the benefit of the Whole,
that "All" who yearned, may find Him!

He Is

Image of the imageless, corp of the incorporeal,
countenance of the faceless, speech of the speechless,
conceivor of the inconceivable.

Fountain of all founts, root of all shoots,
almighty power of existence,
radiance of all radiation,
unconditional lover of all.

Benefactor, who benevolently bestows wisdom
on all those whom He wills to be wise,
force of all those to whom he lends His force,

congregator of all those whom he congregates in His Name.

Revealer of that which He reveals, eye of insightfulness,
breath of all that breathes, life of all that lives,
Oneness of all who dwell in His wholeness.

All live in the unique One, He robes Himself totally
and keeps His single name a secret.
He is indivisible, yet seems to be one thing to one man,
and something else to another;
He is immutable and never changes into mutable forms,
now one thing, now another,
He simply Is beyond Himself, to the uttermost absolute limit
of human understanding.

He is each and every one of the Realms simultaneously,
He is what all of them are,
without actually being anyone of them,
yet immanent in them and transcending them,
there is no place where He is not;
each atom and quark only moves by His Will alone!
His powers and virtues are myriad, silent,
He is the many in the One and the One in the many.

Aeonic Activity

All who issue from Him, aeons from the aeons,
children of His creative nature are also in a creative state,
and honour their Father as He was their primal cause;
He creates His aeons as roots, sources and fathers of all,
they have been born from His knowledge and wisdom,
so they thank and glorify Him, for their birth.

In their hymns of praise and worship,
they combine in a force of unity with one another,
and glorify Him together as a pleromatic congregation.

The perfect Father when He is glorified, hears them
so as He can make them as He, Himself is.
Their second honour is that they all knew His grace
by which they bore fruit with each other.

Because of His will and compassion;
they too, become fathers through the freedom
and power bestowed upon them,
as individually they lack the force to glorify
the One whom they love;
they are flawless and fulfilled
as manifestations of their Father whom they praise.

Through their freedom and the force bestowed upon them

they are called The Third Glory Fathers, as they are glorious,
united, not as individuals, to those they love,
but their fruits are to honour the will of each aeon,
and its qualities;
so there are "nous" of "nous" found to be words of words,
elders of elders, degrees of degrees,
respected one above another.

Each one who bestows glory has his rightful place,
his habitation and haven, which is inherent
in the glory which emanates from Him;
they create everlastingly in the service of assisting one another,
as their emanations are infinite and beyond measurement;
since their Father is never jealous towards those
who issue from Him and create even a manifestation
similar or equal to Him, Himself.

Whoever He wills, He makes a father
of whom He is actually the Real Father and God Almighty;
He makes them Wholes whose entirety He Is!
in the real sense that all the Great Names
are maintained there, names which the angels share,
who have come into existence in the cosmos with the archons.

The complete organisation of the aeons
is unconditional love and yearning for perfection,
that is, the whole knowledge of their Father,

and this is the concordance between them
that has no barrier towards its fulfilment;
although the Father reveals Himself everlastingly,
He doesn't will that they should know Him fully,
as He requires "That" to be sought, for yet keeping
His own inscrutable Primal Being.

For He is our Father,
who grants vital force from His shoot to the root of the aeons,
as there are stations on the way, which lead towards Him,
as if toward a School of Moral Conduct.

He has shown them the possibilities of Great Faith
and earnest prayer to Him, the unseen,
and a sure trust in Him of whom
they are unable to comprehend;
and a burning love, which yearns towards the unknown,
and an acceptable understanding of His eternal "nous"
and grace which is both Providence and Liberation,
as well as knowledge of the One Self of All Beings,
that wills the Father's glory for Himself.

It is by virtue of His will that the Father can be known
through the One Self of All Beings;
the One Self of absolute, pure, unborn,
deathless consciousness that permates the Whole
and fires the search for the Unknown One,

just as one is attracted by a fragrant perfume
to seek out the source from where it springs,
as the scent of our Father is emminently superior
to all other aromas ever breathed by man, woman or beast!

His perfume gives the aeons ineffable delight
and the idea of linking with Him in a united way
is a help for each other in the spirit, planted within them.

Although existing under a burden, they are refreshed,
as it is impossible for them to be alienated
from the source of their Being;
they are silent about His power
and yet receive their form from Him.

They hold Him hidden in a conception
yet maintain silence about His real nature and magnitude,
while it is by the grace of His spirit, which is the scent
of their enquiry into Him and their own true Self,
that He gives them the capacity to comprehend Him;
each aeon is a Name, although they are single,
they are myriad in qualities and names!

The acts of the aeons don't happen
because they are separate from one another!
Their creations are extensions of their united Selves,
just as their Father reaches out to all those whom He loves,

so they might become Him as well.

Just as the current aeon is divided into units of time,
from years into moments,
so this aeon of Truth which is both the One and the many,
is exalted by the greater and lesser Names
according to the ability of each to feed it,
like a spring feeds rivers and lakes,
or a tap root feeds the tree, its branches and fruit,
or the vital energy from the source,
feeds all the body's limbs and organs, great and small,
when awake, and while in deepest sleep.

FLAWED BIRTH OF THE LOGOS

The aeons were Self-originated from the free will
and wisdom which their Almighty Father gave them;
they don't wish to exalt that which issues from a concordance
coming from the worship of each Pleroma;
nor with any other power, above or below,
except for that which might wish to ascend to Him.
So they keep silent about their Father's
unknown inscrutability, yet speak about anyone
who wishes to understand Him.

It once occurred to an aeon
that he should try and understand
the inscrutability of his Father,
as He is a Logos of His own Oneness,
and not emanating from the concordance
among the "Wholes".

This aeon was then given wisdom,
so he could be present prior to each one's conceptions,
as by that which He wills, so will they be made.

Thus he accepted Sage wisdom
in order to study the concealed fundamentals
of his Father's unknowableness;
the free will which was born with the "Wholes"
was the cause of this enquiring aeon,
to permit him to do what he wished, in this respect,
without constraint or restraint for ever more.

The aim of the Logos, who is this aeon,
was well intentioned and benign;
when he began, he worshipped his Father,
even if his attempt might lead to a consequence
beyond the realm of possibility,
but he wanted to create a "flawless one",
from a concordance which hadn't been made
and without it having been ordained.

This aeon was the last made by mutual aid,
and he was of small dimension;
before he could attain any result to exalt his Father's will,
in concordance with the "Wholes",
he acted generously from unconditional love
and commenced to investigate
that which envelops the flawless splendour,
as it wasn't without his Father's will
that this Logos was permitted to progress this far.

The Father had granted him permission
for the benefit of those whom he knew it was right
that they should come into existence;
then the Father and the "Wholes" withdrew
so the boundaries which the Father had set
might be well founded,
and what was "to be" might have a structure,
as it wouldn't come into existence
through the manifestation of the Pleroma.

So it is wrong to be judgemental
about the process which is termed "Logos",
but it is right that we can say that its process
is the root of a foundation pre-ordained to actualise;
the Logos self-originated as it was full and unified,
for the exaltation of its own Father for whom it yearned,
and did so being at peace with itself.

But for those whom he wished to grasp it,
he created in shadows, imitations and similitudes,
as he was incapable of standing the full blaze of the light;
and he peered into the abyss and became doubtful;
there was then a split in his perception,
and he became deeply disturbed,
and then turned outwards,
into forgetfulness of his own Self
and ignorance of "That which he really is".

His self-glorification and hope of comprehending
the incomprehensible became steady,
but the melancholic malaise pursued it
when he strayed beyond himself;
having come into existence through self-doubt;
he failed to reach the throne of the Father's glory,
the One whose high place is boundless;
the Father did not accept him, as he never received Him.

That power which had fashioned this imperfect aeon
 hastened back to his companion in the Pleroma
and then abandoned him because he was imperfect,
and any who had issued from him in this fantastic way,
as they weren't truly his.

When that aeon which had made himself
as potentially perfect did manifest,

he became weak, from his feminine side
which had deserted its strong masculine counterpart;
from this deficiency, more defects came into existence
from his thoughts and pride, and the perfect in him left,
and returned to those who were truly his own;
he remained however, in the Pleroma as a reminder for him,
so that he could eventually turn
and be saved from his mistaken egotism.

Thus the one who raised himself to a higher plane,
and then drew him back to himself was not sterile,
but in creating a fruit in the Pleroma,
he disturbed those trapped by the defect;
the defective were similar to the Pleroma
which issued as egotistic thoughts; shadows, mimicries,
similitudes, and ghosts of qualities in the Pleroma,
lacking reason and light.

They were vain, and the results of nothing that is truly real;
thus their death would be as their birth,
from that which was "nothing"
they would return to non-existence;
on their own they appear greater and more forceful
than their names, which are but shadows;
as mirrored reflections they may seem beautiful,
but alas they are only copies, not originals!

They imagined themselves as self-existent beings,
without need of a source; so they were blind
to any power that was prior to their own existence;
and they lived in a state of rebellion and revolt,
without any humility before their Creator
who had brought them into Being;
they lusted to rule and prevail over each other
in a state of valueless ambition.

While their true nature contained the cause
of that organisation which was eventually to happen,
they were only similitudes of things which are honoured,
brought to a greed for power, in each one,
according to the virtuous name
of which they were only the mere shadow;
each one fantasised it was superior
to its companions and neighbours.

The conception of these phantoms was not sterile,
but like those of which they were imitations,
all that they conceived was manifested as offspring;
many were born as aggressors, faultfinders, and apostates!
They were rebels and power seekers;
all the subsequent generations of these types
emanated from these shadow beings.

The Logos Converted

The Logos was the root cause of all those called into existence
but he continued to be confused and was amazed,
for instead of perfection and flawlessness
he witnessed imperfection and defect;
instead of unification he saw separateness,
and instead of equilibrium he saw instability,
and instead of peace there was turbulence and turmoil.

Nor was it possible to make these creatures
cease wallowing in trouble and disturbance,
nor was it possible for him to end their suffering;
he felt utterly and completely helpless,
now his sense of wholeness and celebration had deserted him;
for those who entered into existence didn't know themselves
and who they really were.

Neither did they know the Pleromas from which they'd issued
nor the One who caused their coming into Being!
This Logos being in such an untenable condition,
stopped creating further emanations,
which were inherent in the Pleroma,
all those splendours which exist to exalt our Father,
instead he produced diminutive frail beings,
handicapped by sickness and disease
from which he suffered too.

It was their similarity to his prime disposition
which had caused all this chaotic instability
which doesn't normally exist in its origin;
then this aeon which had created the imperfection
in these beings who were lacking,
pondered over the situation he'd brought about
by acting irrationally,
and this became a judgement and a condemnation.

He determined to struggle against these results
and tendencies until they were utterly destroyed;
the struggle against these tendencies
which divine wrath pursued and eventually accepts,
forgives them for their errors and rebellion,
and this is the great conversion, termed "metanoia";
the Logos turned to another viewpoint and understanding.

Having turned away from evil, he turned towards the good,
and prayed in gratitude to the One
who had converted him back to goodness;
the One in the Pleroma was the first
to whom he gave thanks and recalled;
he remembered his brothers, individually and collectively,
but before all of them, his Father!

This prayer helped him in his return journey,
and in the Whole, he found the cause

of his ability for Self-remembering
in his own primal existence prior to any manifestation.
This was the thought which, reaching out for him,
brought him back home;
all his prayer and Self-remembering brought many powers
in his consciousness which was no longer sterile.

These powers were good,
and were superior to those of his shadow,
as these often belonged to falsehood and error,
from a delusion of similitude.
For an arrogance had resulted from whence they originated;
these were like Self-forgetfulness, torpor and nightmares;
their opposites were like beings of light, seeking the dawn,
and they sent him dreams which were cosily cheerful
and stopped these nagging thoughts.

Although he was unequal before "That" which pre-existed,
as they were superior to any similitudes,
it was through him, singly,
through which they were more honoured
than those from wicked intentions.
It wasn't from his infirmity
that this goodness came into existence,
but from that in him which sought to find the unborn,
deathless Self of his pre-existence.

Once he earnestly and sincerely prayed,
he lifted himself up, to the good,
and planted in these beings a new tendency to seek
and pray to the glorious pre-existent One!
Together with the notion that they should contemplate
something much greater than their petty little selves,
that which exists prior to them,
although they failed to comprehend what "That" was!

Giving birth to concord and mutual love, through that effort,
they acted as one, since it was from that unity
which they had primarily received their very own existence!
They were mightier than their adversaries,
still in the grip of lust for power,
for they were more exalted than these predecessors;
these lacked humility, and believed they were self-made
without a known source.

What they had produced from this first birth
fought for control,
and became steeped in greed for power and egotism,
and the vain love of glory, without redeeming qualities;
so the "nous" of the Logos once a cause of their creation,
was now wide open to a new revelation of hope,
which would come from above, due to his metanoia.

The Birth of the Saviour

This Logos who lived had the promise
and anticipation of "he" who's honoured;
as for those who walk in the valley of the shadow,
he separated himself, as they opposed him,
and were proud in his sight;
but he was at peace with the beings of good conception,
as are the ones established in his path,
as he is within the sphere of remembering the defective.

The Logos brought him, in an unseen way,
from amongst those who came into existence
until the light shone upon him from above as a giver of Life,
born from brotherly love out of the pre-existent Pleroma.

The failings of the aeons, which did not affect
the Father of the Whole, were brought to him,
as if they were his own, in a careful compassionate way,
so they might be taught about their defect by that unique One,
from whom they accepted the necessary strength
to end their imperfection;
the ordainment which was his came into existence
from him who moved on high,
and which emanated from him and the whole perfection;
for the one who was defective,
an intermediary was needed with the aeons.

When he prayed to them, they gladly agreed
to assist the defective ones;
they all congregated imploring their Father,
with best intentions, that He might help the poor defective,
as they couldn't become perfected, in any other way,
unless it was His will;
from this joyful harmony they willed the fruit,
a Oneness revealing their Father's face,
whom the aeons had implored
as they prayed for aid for their imperfect brother.

And the Father was with them,
and acknowledged His agreement of union with them,
which is the beloved Son;
the Son in whom the Whole is delighted,
put himself on them as one would a robe,
by which he bestowed his perfection upon the defective,
and gave affirmation to those already perfect.

This One, properly named the Saviour,
Redeemer, Beloved, and Christ,
Light of the Elect, to whom our prayers are offered;
but what better name may be to him than the Son,
as he is the knowledge of his Father,
that which he wished them to realise.

So not only did the aeons bring forth

their Father's face whom they worship,

but they also created their own countenances;

they became a force for Him, as for a King,

since the beings of this conception

share a strong fellowship and harmonious relationship;

they emanated in many-sided forms,

so that the one who was to be helped,

might know those to whom he prayed,

and the One who bestowed it on him.

The fruit of this concordance with the Father,

He made subject to the authority of the Wholes,

for our Father has placed the Wholes within Himself,

those which pre-existed, the ones present now,

and the ones yet to be;

the Father ordained His Creation,

so He commenced and effected His great revelation!

The One in whom the Father is,

and the One in whom the Wholes are,

pre-existed before the Son.

The Father taught His Son

about those who searched for truth,

by means of the shining of that radiant beacon light;

He perfected him in unspeakable joy,

for Himself as a flawless one,

and He showed him what was fitting to give each soul.

This is the primal joy, and He planted in him a Word,
unseen, which is predetermined to be Self Knowledge;
and He gave him the power to divide
and throw out from himself those who rebelled against him;
but to those who entered existence because of him,
He revealed a form far surpassing them all;
sometimes they behaved in an opposing manner,
one to another, so He came to them as a lightning flash!
and ended their embroilments.

They were frightened and prostrated since they were unable
to stand the radiance of the light which had struck!
Later they welcomed his intervention and worshipped him,
becoming his witnesses; they accepted his light
as being stronger than those who opposed him.

But the beings of the shadows were very afraid,
since they were ignorant of this vision,
and they fell down into the pit of nescience,
the outer darkness, chaos, Hell, and the Abyss;
they were fit to rule over their world of ignorance
as it was their destiny,
but they would be of use in the days to come.

There is a vast distinction between the revelation
of the One who entered into Being to the defective one,
and those yet to come into existence as a result;

for he revealed himself to him, within him,
since he is with him, a fellow sufferer, who gives him peace,
little by little, nourishes his growth, raises him up,
and bestows the joy of vision!

But to those who fall, he shows himself quickly,
then withdraws, only giving them a brief glimpse.

Pleroma of the Logos

When the Logos which was imperfect
became enlightened, his Pleroma began;
he fled from those who had troubled him,
he detached himself from them; he shed his egotism,
he associated with those who had rebelled
after they humbly repented;
and he welcomed ministration
from his brothers who visited him.

He praised all those who had helped him, with gratitude,
as he'd been saved from the rebellion against him,
and admired his allies' valour in coming to his aid.

He created representations of their living faces,
which were pleasant in goodness and beauty,
but unequal in truth since they hadn't yet reached

a concordance between their maker
and the One who had revealed himself to him.

In his wisdom and knowledge he acted,
mingling as Logos with his true Self completely;
thus all those who issued from him were magnificent
as "that which is" is magnificent!

He was astonished at the glorious splendour
of those who appeared before him;
he gave thanks for their visitation;
the Logos carried out these deeds
through those who had helped him
for the establishment of those
who had entered existence because of him,
and so they would receive grace,
as he prayed for them to be well ordered
so they might reach balance.

Thus those he consciously created rode in chariots,
so they could move through spheres below them;
and find their rightful place in harmony with their true nature.

This is catastrophe for beings of the shade,
yet is a deed of benevolence for the beings of the light;
the children of light emanate
from an ordainment which is unified;

while they may have suffered, they flower from seeds,
and have not come to Be by their own self-will alone.

The One who appeared was a face from the Father,
and harmonious.
He wore a beautiful robe of every grace and nurture
which serves all those from the Logos,
emerging while in prayer and worship;
they are the ones whom he exalted,
regarding their heartfelt prayer,
so he might perfect them
through the symbols he'd created.

So the Logos added even more to their joint aid and hope
as they are content, at peace, and enjoy pure pleasure;
he created those he recalled first, while they were absent,
having recognised their perfection.

Even now, those whom he remembers
shall live in the flawless Father,
as much as in the Wholes;
he appears to him before he consorts with his soul,
so that what has come into being
might not be lost by looking at the light,
for they find it difficult to accept this high exaltation.

The "nous" of the Logos who had returned to equilibrium,

reigned over those who had entered existence because of him,
and were named "aeon" and "place";
it's sometimes named the "Temple of Salvation"
because he healed himself from identification
with a myriad thought patterns, and through grace
returned to the single thought of God, Self or Saviour
which are synonymous in this text.

Sometimes it's named "The Storehouse",
because of the fruits he gathered for himself alone;
sometimes it's named "The Bride",
because of the holy joy of the One
who gave himself to his or her soul,
in the hope of offspring from the marriage.

It's sometimes named "The Kingdom"
because of its stability and the triumphant joy of victory
over the tendencies which struggled against him or her;
sometimes it's named "The Joy of God"
because of the rejoicing in which he robed himself.

With him is the eternal light giving reward
for the goodness within him
and his earnest desire for liberation and freedom.

The aeon is above the two orders
of those who struggle one with the other;

it isn't a friend of those who hold power
and isn't involved in the feebleness and frailty
belonging to dark thoughts and the shadow side!
That aeon in which the Logos established himself
was ineffable blissful joy;
so beautiful aeon was a reflection
of all that subsists in the Pleroma.

The face of the One who revealed himself
was rich in earnest sincerity,
power of attention, and the hope of salvation,
and all for which he yearned, prayed and sought!;
his countenance had the mark of the Son,
his essence, power and form,
the one who he loved and with whom he was pleased.

It was light and a wish to be settled;
it was open to learn the teaching
and possessed a visionary eye; it was also wise
in its opposition to the shadow world below;
it was a Word for utterance
and creating perfection where needed.

And many took form from the likeness of the Pleroma,
as from their fathers who gave them life,
each one being an image of one of its facets.
These are forms of brave masculinity

and aren't sprung from the effeteness in femininity.

It's named "The Church", for in concord, they're like
the concordance of those in his congregation
who have revealed themselves.

That which came into existence
from the semblance of the light,
that too is flawless, as it is an image
of the one great, primordial, existing,
eternal light, which constitutes "the Wholes".

Even if it's less, as a likeness of "That",
it still has indivisibility
as it is a facet of primal indivisible light;
but those who entered existence
in the semblance of an aeon,
are similar in essence, but unequal in power;
in association with each other they're equal,
but each hasn't yet cast off its own idiosyncracy
and passions remain.

They're a defect as they don't emanate
from the concordance of the Pleroma,
but arise prematurely before his acceptance of the Father;
but this agreement with His Wholeness and Will
was good for the structures to come;

it was made possible for them to move in the lower places;
these places can only endure their coming singly;
a necessary visitation for all to be eventually perfected.

So the Logos received his universal vision;
that which pre-existed, that which is present now,
and that which shall be, since he has been entrusted
with the ordainment of all that exists;
some essences are already inherent
in that which is ready to enter being,
and the seeds he holds within himself;
he produces his offspring as a revelation, from his thought.

The seed of his promise is kept, so that those to come
for a mission in the world may be sent,
through the blessed advent of Christ the Saviour,
his disciples, apostles, and saints;
these are the ones who are first in Divine Self Knowledge,
that they and the Father are One,
and so realise the full majesty, glory, and splendour
of their everloving Father and King.

Government of the Material World

It is appropriate from the earnest prayer
implored by the Logos and his metanoia
which came, through God's grace,
as a consequence that some would perish,
some flourish, and others set aside;
he first prepared the chastisement of the rebellious,
using the power of he who had authority over "All",
so as to be distinguished from him.

He is the One beneath who keeps himself separate
from that which is honoured,
until he creates the structure of all that's outside,
and gives to all and everything its proper place;
this Logos first stabilised himself
when he beautified the Wholes,
both as a cardinal principle but as an organic cause,
a Lord of all which would manifest, like his Father.

He made pre-existent forms, in gratitude and glorification,
and beautified the home of those brought forth in honour,
called Paradise or "The Enjoyment",
which holds the form of all the goodness of the Pleroma;
then he beautified the Kingdom, like a City
filled with delight, fraternal love, infinite generosity
and the Holy Spirit which the Logos placed in Lordship.

Then he consecrated the Church
which congregates there from the form
pre-existent in the aeon, exalting our Father;
then he beautified the home of great Faith,
submission arising from hope,
revealed when the Light appeared!
Then he beautified the place of prayer and supplication,
followed by mercy and forgiveness,
and the prophecy of the One to come.

All spiritual domains rest in divine power,
they're distinct from creatures
dependent on conceptual thought,
since the power is established in a form
which divides the Pleroma from the Logos;
that prophetic power directs conceptual creatures
who are moving towards knowledge
of the pre-existent Selfhood,
but doesn't allow them to see all their powers.

These beings still dependent on conceptualisation
of the external are humbled,
they keep the remembrance of the Pleroma,
as they share in the names by which all is made
sublime and beautiful! Metanoia humbles them,
and the Judgement is merciful towards them.

Also humbling is the power which divides
those who fall beneath them, and sends them far away
and doesn't permit them to influence the converted.
They're still lost in fear, confused, Self-forgetful,
bewildered and ignorant, living in fantasy;
they even give these dark states of arrogance, greed for power,
lust, rebellion, and lies, various exalted names.

For each the Logos gave a Name,
those belonging to the converted are "The Right Ones",
the Intuitive, the Fiery, and Intermediate;
the arrogant are called The Left-Handed,
Hylic, Dark Ones and the Last.
After the Logos had set each soul in its rightful place,
the forms and the shadows,
he kept the aeon pure from all the forces which oppose it,
as it is a home of celebration and rejoicing.

However, for those still in bondage to conceptual thought,
so that they might find the will to diminish their egotism,
and might see the disease which makes them suffer,
and search for their own true Self of Love,
after continuous enquiry,
this will heal them of their infirmity.

Those souls who belonged to the conversion,
he set in the charm of beauty to bring them into form;

then he set them over the law of judgement,
and over the powers which their egotism had produced
in their greed for power and fame.

He set them up as governors over the fallen,
so either by the charm of beauty, threat of law,
or their desire for power, order might be regained
from those who had reduced it to wickedness;
the Logos was pleased with them
as they helped to order the structure;
he gave to each a station to rule;
consequently they became his captains and lieutenants.

In places of rule, even angels and archangels submitted,
each one of these archons with his breed and qualities
was a guardian entrusted with maintaining order
in the structure; none are without Rulers
from the end of the heavens to the ends of the earth,
and in the nether worlds;
there are always those who give commands
to administer chastisement, justice, giving rest,
healing, education and protection.

Over all the archons there was a Chief Archon,
the aspect which the Logos conceived
as a representation of the Father of the Wholes;
so he is decorated with splendid names like father,

god, demiurge, king, and judge;
he is the strong right hand of the Logos
to beautify and craft in the sphere below,
and was the chosen voice to issue prophecy
from the Logos himself.

When he saw that the words were auspicious
he rejoiced as if they were his own utterances,
not realising that he was a channel for the spirit of the Logos;
he also worked as father of the ordainment
and created by his own elected spirit,
original words which were from the Spirit.

Since essentially he was a god and father
he felt these were his own elements,
and established peace for the obedient
and suffering for the rebellious.
With him there was also a Paradise and a kingdom
which exists in the aeon which pre-existed him;
these were more precious than his copies
which were like shadows and a robe,
because he failed to understand the way
in which things that exist, actually do exist!

He employed craftsmen and servants to help him in his task,
for wherever he worked he left his imprint of beauty;
he set up emblems of light, spiritually from his own essence,

exalted by him in each place;
purity, paradises, kingdoms, havens of rest
and lords of dominions, subservient to his will.

After they had heard about the great Light
which is the source of "All"
he set them over the beauty unfolding below;
the unseen spirit impelled him
so that he could rule through his own servant,
whom he used as his good right hand
and a clear voice, as if he wore his face.

This servant brings order through awe, so the ignorant
might fear the commandments given them to keep,
as they're chained firmly in the bonds of the archons.

This whole material order is in three divisions;
the strong forces which the spiritual Logos brought out
from fantasy and pride, were in the first rank;
then powers brought out of their greed for power
were in the middle; these were forces of ambition
so they might rule the dominions beneath them.

Those which emerged from envy and similar traits
he set in a subservient rank, governing the boundaries,
from which came diseases;
thus he appointed governing powers

acting on the world of gross materiality,
that the offspring of those which endured there
might continue to exist forever;
this was the structure of order that the Logos established.

THE CREATION OF HUMANITY

The conception which lies between the sides
of right or light and left or dark, is a power of creation;
all those which the primordial ones wish to form
are a projection of their own, like a bodily shadow;
these are the root causes of visible manifestations;

Thus the whole illusion of the world
as representation or as moving pictorial images,
has come into being because of those souls
which needed education and reformation,
so that the "small" might grow, little by little,
as through a mirror reflection of the ideal.

For this purpose he finally created mankind,
having first set in order Nature,
which would supply all his needs;
for the creation of mankind, the Logos moved in him, "unseen",
as he perfected them through the Demiurge and his angels,
who shared the task after he conferred with his archons.

Man is like a shadow, as he is exiled from the Wholes,
but he is formed by all the forces
both of the right and left sides;
but the form which the Logos made was imperfect
as it wasn't a true likeness of himself,
as it was fashioned somewhat forgetfully and weakly.

This was because the Logos entrusted the primal form
to the Demiurge, out of nescience,
so he would learn that the Honoured One truly lives
and he would learn that he needs him;
this is what the prophets called "Living Spirit"
of honoured aeons and the unseen;
this is the living soul which gives life its power,
but was dead at first in ignorance.

The Soul of the first man is from the spiritual Logos,
while the creature thinks it is his,
as it seems to be a part of him, like the nose which breathes.
The Logos sent down souls from his substance
since he has the power of generation
because he emanates from his Father's image.
The left-handed also issued some men,
as they've the shadow power of Being.

Spiritual substance is unique, and a single image,
its weakness is its division into different forms;

psychics aren't inclined to wickedness;
materialists have many forms, which is a defect,
and the soul suffers from many different tendencies;
the first man is a mixed form,
both from the left and the right hand,
and his attention is divided between the opposites.

It is said that a paradise was planted deep inside his heart,
with three trees, so he could eat three different fruits,
since it's a garden of three different orders,
and this is what gives him delight;
the noble inclination in him was more honoured,
it could make, but not wound!

So they threatened him with peril, which is death;
for he was permitted only to eat the wicked fruit
and not from the other tree,
nor from the tree of everlasting life,
as they were tempted by the cunning serpent;
he led man astray to follow his wandering thoughts
and perverted desires; he disobeyed the command
so he should die and was expelled.

It is a sign, that it is a short time before mankind
will receive the enjoyments of the eternal good.
This was his plan that man should first experience
the great evil of spiritual death,

a total ignorance of the Whole,
and he should suffer the consequences,
and then receive the greatest good of firm Self Knowledge
of the Whole and eternal life;
because the first man erred, death reigned,
it is used to kill each man in its kingdom,
because of the Father's will.

DIFFERENT BELIEFS

If both polarities of the "left hand" and "right hand"
are brought together by the idea which is between them,
and gives them their structure, they both act in a similar way,
the right resembling the left, and vice versa.

At times the wicked order does evil in a stupid way,
and the wise order emulates the violent man,
even performing occasional wicked deeds.

Sometimes the foolish order wants to do good deeds,
imitating real goodness in an eager way!
the consequences are often disastrous!

Scholars have argued endlessly about the cause of existence
and why things are exactly as they are.
Some claim it is all due to Divine Providence,

as they see equilibrium and order
in the motion of the Creation.

Others say it is alienated from the Divine
because they see barbarism and dark powers at work;
others are Determinists and say everything which exists
is predestined by the Divine Will,
and can't be different from "what it is"!

These people are obsessed by material universe
based on sensual evidence only;
others say it is in accord with a mysterious Nature
which is a powerful force;
others say it is Self-existent and inscrutable!

The vast majority only see the visible elements
and don't have a deeper more perceptive knowledge!
Those who are wise amongst the Greeks and Pagans
put forward fanciful theories about various powers,
brought into being from their own imagination
and vain thought!

They're usually highly argumentative
and indulge in conflict and rebellion!
They're often arrogant in their opinions,
for they describe only shadows and appearances
which deceive them and they fall into error

because of all these varying beliefs.

The order was always disputing amongst itself
and was led by the arrogant offspring of an archon!

So there was disagreement about philosophy, medicine,
rhetoric, music, logic and scientific theory;
a Tower of Babel ensued because of all these champions
of different points of view!

As for the knowledge of the Jews
who spoke in the style of the Platonists,
these righteous ones searched to find the truth
and used the mixed powers within them.

Eventually they reached the order of Purified Ones,
those that established the Oneness of Divine Unity
as an image of their Father.
This conception is not invisible but wisdom pervades it,
so it images the form of the Unseen One;
consequently some angels fail to comprehend it.

The Jews, the Righteous Ones, and their Prophets
never thought of anything nor said anything
from imagination or from esotericism,
but by the powers at work within them
while attending to that which they contemplated,

reaching a vision of cosmic harmony.

But there is one even greater than these wise savants,
who was appointed, as they needed him,
by the spiritual Logos himself,
who sowed the seed of salvation.

His was an enlightening Word;
as the Righteous Jews preserved the tradition
of their Prophets and testimony
concerning the One who is Great, honoured by their fathers,
who were yearning to hear His Word.

In them the seed of worship and enquiry
was strongly sown; it drew them to love,
with all their souls, minds and hearts, the exalted One!;
and to preach all that pertained to his essential Unity,
one without a second.
This was a Unity which worked through them
as they preached; their vision and testimony was unanimous
and didn't differ amongst them;
so those who have studied their words accept their scriptures,
but interpreting them somewhat differently.

Through misinterpretation they established errors
which currently exist amongst some Jews;
they claim their God is One

who spoke in the ancient scriptures,
but at the same time was just the single mind in Nature.

Others claim his work is linked with
the creation of good and evil powers,
others that he is the creator of all which manifests,
from angels to devils;
a multiplicity of different ideas and commentaries
were written by teachers of this law.

The Prophets, on the other hand,
never spoke from their own notions,
but only what they had seen
and heard through the Messiah.

Many prophesied the advent of the Messiah
who is our Saviour;
none knew exactly when he would come
and from whom he would be born;
the Saviour alone is the only one able to speak
about his origin and mission.

He is an unbegotten child
from the spiritual Logos who entered a body;
his body was conceived, in the seed state,
at the unveiling of the Primal Light,
according to his Father's will.

For the Son that lives is not a seed of the mundane,
but the son of the one, whom the Father ordained
for this miracle of his salvation!

To that one belonged all that was needed
to create his entry into the world as his Father willed;
his Father's one and alone, unseen, inscrutable,
who is God in this form so he might be known!

THE SAVIOUR AND HIS FRIENDS

He is our Saviour born from boundless compassion.
It is for our sake that he came into the world of dark sorrow
and suffered involuntarily.

He became flesh, blood and eternal Soul
nothing corruptible could endure within his divine nature.
And for those that had ears to hear his words
this unseen one taught them in an unseen way
from and about himself.

He took upon the shoulders of his perfected Self
the burden of death of all those he strove to save
accepting their poverty of spirit
into which they had fallen at birth in a body
because he too had been conceived

as a babe in a body and soul.

Amongst those who shared and praised him
and received his gift of light,
he was greatly honoured as he was born,
without sin, flaw or blemish,
into this arduous valley of the shadows
which is full of passion and changing opinion,
from the Great Logos who moved,
and established all creatures
with their unique bodies and souls.

He entered existence and being
from the splendour of a glorious vision
and the unchanging "nous" of the Logos
who returned back to his own divine Self
from his pre-ordained structure,
as those who come, take on a body and soul;
as an affirmation of all that is its essential stability
and eventual judgement.

When they remembered the Saviour
they came to him, and he knew;
those were more honoured,
who were drawn by his emanation in the flesh,
than those who had come suffering from some defect,
although they were all substantially the same,

their dispositions are different;

Some came to him from passion
and a sense of separation, and needed healing;
and some came from prayer that they might heal the sick,
when they're called to treat those who have fallen;
these are the apostles and evangelists,
disciples of the Saviour and teachers who need guidance.

Why did all these share the passions of the body?
Because unlike the Saviour they weren't a symbol
of that One who is the "All" in bodily form.

Instead they were symbols of all in creation,
so they assume a pose of separation taken from the pattern,
having entered a form for the germination
of all that exists beneath the heavens.

This is what shares in the evil
which lives in the realms they have inhabited;
as The Will held the Whole under defect
so that by His Will, He might have mercy on the "All".

Thus His eventual salvation is assured,
while a unique Saviour is given eternal Life
and the others need salvation;
so from this power they received great gifts of grace

granted by Lord Jesus; this was proclaimed to his flock,
since the seed of Christ's promise of revelation
and union, had been established.

This promise embraced the teaching
of the return journey from where they were
to what they would become through his grace;
this is redemption!

It is release from bondage and total acceptance of freedom;
without this redemption the captivity of those
who are slaves of ignorance is held by hypnotic power;
this freedom is Knowledge of the Divine Self
which pre-existed before the fall into the pit of nescience.

This freedom is forever, and is real salvation
from the servile bondage which they have suffered;
even those who have been brought down
through vain egotism and thoughts which attract them
towards evil and greed for power,
may receive this freedom from the abundance of his grace,
which shows mercy on all his children.

They suffered from a turmoil of passions and desires
brought about by the destruction of all that was thrown off
when the Logos separated from himself;
the Logos who was the cause of their fall

kept them at the end of the ordered structure
and allowed them to exist
as they were helpful for that which was ordained.

We now turn attention to the three essential types
which constitute mankind.

THREE TYPES OF MEN AND WOMEN

There are three types of men and women,
the spiritual, psychological and materialistic;
these conform with the triple disctinctions
inherent in the Logos,
from which they issued.

Each type is known by its works,
but they weren't recognised until the advent of the Saviour
who shone brilliantly among the saints
and revealed the essence of each mental condition.

The spiritual breed were like light
from the light of the spirit and when the Son appeared
they rushed towards him instantly;
they became body and limbs to his head and heart;
they immediately received the knowledge of his revelation.

The psychological are like firelight,
as they hesitate in accepting the knowledge he revealed,
and they lack faith.
They're taught through an inner voice,
and this is adequate since it's not far away
from the hope of his promise;
since they received as a pledge his assurance of what was to be.

The materialist breed is, however, altogether foreign,
as it is dark; it avoids the shining of the light
because it promises to destroy its wilfulness and egotism,
since they haven't yet seen its promise of unification,
and they end up despising the Lord because of his revelation.

The spiritual will soon receive salvation
while the materialists will receive destruction
while they resist him;
the psychological are in the middle, as they're divided
between, pure and impure tendencies;
but through determined struggle,
and a strong desire for freedom,
the strong make the necessary effort;
then when the time is ripe,
they suddenly escape from the repetitive dismal dream of life.

So those whom the Logos created from his primal conception,
when his own Self remembered the honoured One

and yearned for freedom, received salvation immediately;
all men and angels can be saved, if they follow his lead.

Those who are saved by effort and grace
are appointed to serve in announcing
the advent of our Saviour and his revelation;
whether men, women, or angels,
when he was sent as a help to them,
they learned to know the Divine Self of their own Being;
but those emanating from lust for power
came from the blows of those who battle against him.

They're in between good and evil
and will perish suddenly until they turn
and seek the kingdom of heaven within their hearts;
they'll be delivered from their greed for power
and will praise the Lord who will end his wrath
and reward them for their egolessness, which will stay for ever.

But those wallowing in their ambition for power
who fail to recognise the teaching of the Son of God
will receive judgement for their folly and ignorance
which is continued suffering until they return.

Some who strayed, even exceeded their own wickedness
and with the left-handed dark forces conspired for his death;
they determined they could become the kings of the universe,

if the real Christ the King was slain.

They worked to achieve this aim,
that is those men and angels
not living from their good right-handed nature,
but from some bizarre mixture.

They chose to be exalted amongst men which is temporary,
instead of willing the way to everlasting peace, by selflessness
and striving for the salvation of their fellow men and women,
living from righteousness.

After their repentence they reflect
on how they can best serve the Church
and her fellow members, sharing in their toil and suffering.

This contrasts with men of the left-hand path
who follow the way of falsehood
and plot against the Church and her sanctity;
and this is the reason for their condemnation,
insofar as they moved to trouble and try the Church.

REDEMPTION

The Elect or Chosen Ones share their body-minds
and souls with the Saviour; for to be with him,
is like being in the Bridal Chamber
because of the "union" and total concordance with him.

Before all else Christ came for the sake of the penitent soul,
and this marriage leads to rejoicing at the Wedding Feast;
all celebrate and are glad, at the union of the Self of Christ
Consciousness, the bridegroom, and the purified soul, the bride!

The chamber is the aeon of reflections,
where the Logos is yet to unite with the Pleroma;
the good repentant man or woman of the Church is ecstatic,
as he or she had prayed, for their exiled spirit,
soul and body to become reunited within her or him
as the Whole and he or she is all of "That which I am"!

When the redemption was proclaimed,
the perfect man knew immediately,
so as to go back quickly to his unified state,
and return joyously from where he first came;
his Church members, needed a hall of learning
"a decorated place" so they could learn from their likenesses,
symbols and archetypes as in a mirror,
and receive their restorative redemption.

This is simultaneous when they have manifested
as the Whole and united with the Pleroma.
There is an initial agreement with the Father,
until the Whole receives its face according to His Will;
redemption or restoration is final
after the Whole reveals itself as the Son,
who is the redemption and the way to our inscrutable Father,
the recollection of our Divine Self, our true nature,
the indescribable pre-existent One.

Thus restoration and redemption are realised!
It wasn't only freedom from the mental tyranny
of the left-handed ones, nor was it in any way
a release from the forces of the right-handed ones;
to each of which we imagine we were slaves,
and from whom escape is difficult,
without being captured once again.

The redemption is an ascent to the heights of the Pleroma,
and to those Named according to the force of each aeon;
it is an entry into profound silence
where there is no need for speech, nor conceptual thought,
but where all is Light which is Self-effulgent!
Not only humans, but also angels need redemption
from the mirror of the aeon's Pleromas and their brilliant
powers of light;

Thus there are no doubts in respect of even the Son himself,
who has the place of Redeemer of the Whole;
he who had become a man when he sacrificed himself
for all we need, we of the flesh, in his Church!

Now he himself also received redemption
from the Word which descended upon him;
then all the rest received redemption through him,
that is all those who had taken him to themselves;
for those who accepted the One who had received redemption,
also received what was in him.

Among men and women born into bodies,
redemption commenced by His Father's first-born,
the embodied Son;
the heavenly angels asked to cooperate with him on Earth.

So he is named "The Redemption Of His Father's Angels",
the Comforter of those striving earnestly
under the whole for his Divine Self Knowledge,
as he was given grace in the first place;
his Father's foresight knew him
before he came into Being when first conceived;
and there were those to whom the Father revealed His son.

He set a lack of understanding on the One who remains
for a certain time as glory for his Pleroma,

since through his "unknowingness"
there was caused the Son's existence;
just as acceptance of knowledge concerning the Son
is a manifestation of his lack of jealousy,
and reveals the magnitude of his sweetness, His second glory;
so He has been found to be a cause of nescience
although He is the fount of Self Knowledge!

In His concealed and inscrutable wisdom,
He held back His knowledge
until the Wholes became tired of seeking Him,
their Father the Divine Self,
whom nobody can find by their own mental effort,
without His Grace!
He gives Himself so they might receive Self Knowledge
of His great glory, and boundless blessing.

He reveals Himself eternally to those who are worthy,
unknown in His essence,
so they might receive Self Knowledge of Him,
through His will that they should yearn to return
after experiencing the pain and suffering brought about
by their dark ignorance and nescience.

Those whom He first conceived
as being fit for Divine Self Knowledge,
and were searching for Truth and Goodness,

the benign wisdom of their Father
saw that they should experience suffering
as a spur for training themselves
in such a way that they might eventually
know their True nature
and receive His glory forevermore!

They regarded their inward enemies
as an aid to struggle against and surmount,
and to see that the ignorance of their Father
and forgetfulness of Self had been their own condition too.

That which gave them knowledge of Him
and their own Self was a power to help them gain
the "knowledge of all that which is thought", "the treasure",
"the revelation of all that was originally known".
"The way of harmonious growth
towards the primordial One",
which is the gain of all those
who have renounced their conceit
which they presumed in their wilfulness,
so that the end might be like the beginning.

As for the great baptism into which the Wholes will descend,
this is the redemption into God, Father, Son and Holy Spirit,
when affirmation is made through strong undivided faith
in those holy names, which are the one name of the Gospel.

From this they receive salvation reaching in an unseen way
the Holy Trinity in undoubting faith!
And when they have testified
it is with the strong certainty that they knew them,
so that the return to them might be witnessed
as the perfection of all those who believe,
and that the Father might be One with them;
the same Father, the God whom they have affirmed in faith
and who bestowed on them union with Himself
through their own Self Knowledge.

The Great Baptism is called "the Robe"
for those who don't remove it from themselves
and for those who wear it, and for those who are redeemed;
it's also termed "Confirmation of Truth Without a Fall",
as in a strong, motionless way
it seizes those who have received redemption.

Baptism is also termed "Silence"
because of its quietness and peace,
and the "Bridal Chamber" because of the marriage
and the indivisible state of those
who know they have known Him!
It is also the "The Flameless Light Which Never Sets"
as those who wear the Robe are transformed into light;
it is also termed "The Eternal Life" which is deathless.

It is also called simply "That Which Is"!
What else is there to call it except for "God"!
since it is all the Wholes,
even if called a thousand names

Just as He transcends every word,
He transcends every voice, mind, the all, and the silence;
so it is with those who are simply "That Which Is".
This is how we find it to be, unspeakable
and inscrutable in its appearance, as it is the advent of Being
in those who know through Him,
and understand, He is the one who they worship.

So concludes the section on Redemption.
The Vocation ends the book.

VOCATION

On this question of "Election"
and those whom are chosen by a "Call"
there are points to make clear;
all who emerge from the Logos
either from "Judgement of Evil Ones"
or "Divine Anger" which opposes them,
and then leads to a return to the Honoured Ones,
from worship and recollection of their Pre-Existent Self,

or great faith and hope in their eventual salvation,

are beings who emerge from the good side,

since their reason for being

came from the One that truly exists.

LETTER TO FLORA

This philosophic epistle to a Christian lady called Flora is by the
Roman Valentinian Scholar Ptolemy. It is in ancient Greek and
was written circa AD 135–185. The question of the authorship of the
Hebrew Pentateuch, and the validity of the Mosaic Revelation, was a
vexatious question among the early Christians. From a Gnostic
standpoint Ptolemy elucidates the solution for the benefit of his pupil.

My dear sister in Christ, Flora,
The Law revealed by the Prophet Moses,
has been greatly misunderstood by many folk,
for they never knew Moses nor the Land of Israel
nor even kept any of his religious rules.

I'm sure you'll agree with me,
if you study the opposing views on this vexed question;
many swear that the Law was given to Moses,
by God, others swear, "twas the work of the devil!"
and think that the Creation is a devilish work.

In my view both sides are utterly wrong!
and fail to see the truth about these books.
It doesn't seem all these Laws were revealed

by a perfect God and ever loving Father, for then,
they must be of the same nature as their author.

In fact they're imperfections,
and needed to be added to by another hand,
and even contain rules which lack concord
with the will of such a perfect God and Father.

And to attribute these Laws to the Devil,
that actually condemns the Devil's injustice is false logic,
and shows that these battlers,
fail to understand the truths of our Saviour.

For Our Lord, Jesus Christ, clearly stated,
"that a house divided against itself must fall!"

What's more, our inspired Apostle John,
affirms that the Creation is truly God's
and that "all things were made by Him,
and without Him, nothing was ever made",
destroying their logic of blasphemy.

Obviously the Creation is by a God who's Just,
and fiercely hates Evil!
not a wicked one, as believed by fools.

They fail to see the kind providence

of our Divine Creator of His world,
and are afflicted by chronic blindness
in the inner eye of their impure souls,
and even in their myopic body's sight!

It must now be very clear to you dear friend,
that these opposing foes are both in error,
and that each one falls
in its own special, idiosyncratic way.

One side's obviously unfamiliar
with our Lord God of Righteousness,
the other, is regrettably unacquainted
with Lord Jesus Christ, Father of All,
who came into Being and Existence,
through His own Almighty God alone,
and who alone was able to know Him.

So it falls to the grateful lot of you and I,
who've been deemed to be fit of receiving
this knowledge of God and Christ,
to show exactly what kind of Law
this Mosaic Code really is,
and who the Law Maker really was.

I shall offer proofs of my case
by quoting Christ's own words,

by which it's only possible
to reach a definite understanding
of truth without falling headlong
into the deep ditch of delusion.

First of all you must see, in its whole,
the Laws of Moses are not spoken by a single voice;
by this I mean, not by God alone;
it's very plain that many of these commands
were formed by human thought.

Christ's words teach us that the Law
is divided into three separate parts.
The first belongs to God, Himself, and His Laws,
while a second belongs
to the prophet Moses and his Laws,
and a third to the Elders of Israel,
who in the very beginning
must have inserted certain
of their own special ideas.

Moses himself ordained
that certain commandments,
were not as God revealed,
but based upon his own views.

I'll tell you how this can be observed

from Jesus Christ's own words.
When Jesus was speaking with priests
who disputed with him about divorce,
and its being allowed in the Torah
he said, "for your stiffness of heart,
Moses permitted divorce of a wife,
but in the beginning, this wasn't so,
for God, Himself, has made this union
and what the Lord has joined together
let no man dare to put asunder!"

Jesus shows that God's Law is one thing
while the Mosaic Law is another
so Moses legislates contrary to God.

But if we examine Moses's aim
in proclaiming this command,
we find he ordained it, not from whim,
but out of need, because the Israelites
were weak and unable to perform God's will!

Some were on bad terms with their wives
and risked inflicting injury and harm on them
so hurting themselves and each other.

The compassionate Moses wishing to rid
his flock from this self-destruction

passed a secondary law of divorce
choosing the lesser of the two evils,
so if they failed to follow God's law,
they could at least keep his provision,
to avoid the shameful consequences.

In this way Moses ordered laws
different from God's specific will.
Christ also shows that the Elders
took a hand in shaping the Law.

Christ said, "God commanded us
to honour our Fathers and Mothers
that it may be well with us!"

But the Elders have said,
"What you would have gained
from me is given to God,"
and for the sake of tradition
these Elders have nullified God's law!

For the Prophet Isaiah said,
"this people honour me with lips
but their hearts are far from me
in vain do they worship my name
teaching as doctrine, notions of men."

So we see that the Law is in three,
from God, Moses and the Elders,
and we've made this sufficiently clear.

What's more my dear, the Laws from God
are also divided into parts of three;
first there are the pure commandments
unmixed with any trace of wickedness.

This is the true law which our Lord
came to fulfil, not to destroy,
for what he fulfilled wasn't estranged
but in need of perfecting through him.

Next is the part mixed with injustice,
which the Lord Jesus ruled against
as salient to his own divine nature.

Thirdly there's the emblematic
after the image of the spiritual sphere
which Christ transformed by parable
from the sensually perceived visible world
to the unseen, subtle, spiritual sphere.

The Ten Commandments are pure but imperfect,
and needed fulfilment by Christ;
that which also lack perfection

are the laws of compensation for harm,
such as "an eye for an eye"
and a "tooth for a tooth".

Here the second, to act unjustly
also acts unjustly with the same deed.

However, this law has a certain virtue
because of the weaknesses of those
to whom it was originally decreed;
yet it's out of character with the nature
of pure love and goodness of our Father.

This law was a result of necessity,
for when God doesn't wish even one murder
proclaiming "thou shalt not kill!"
He ordains a secondary law
sentencing the murderer to death,
acting as judge between two deaths.

Thus He who forbids even one murder
is prevented by sheer necessity;
so His Son when he comes from Him
abolished this injunction, while still admitting
the law belonged to God.

As Lord Jesus says, "For God said;
'he who speaks evil of father or mother
let him die!'" and the same elsewhere.

Now we'll proceed to the emblematic.

Our Lord's, Disciples and Apostles
made these parables widely known
among the multitude, through his words
which are well recorded in their Gospels.

You may well enquire, my dear Flora,
what kind of Being is our God
who ordained these Commands?

He is the Creator of the Universe
and of all things that exist within it.
As Perfection he is wholly good,
yet judge and intermediary
between His goodness and evil.

The essence of the evil adversary
is corruption and darkness,
ignorance and nescience,
impurity and materialism.

While our Father is flawless perfection,
absolute, pure Self-existent light,
simple, clear and perfectly unique.

In my next letter, my dear Flora
I'll tell you how these differences
between Good and Evil arose
according to our Gnostic tradition.

With love, from your brother in Christ.

Ptolemy

PETER AND
THE PEARL SELLER

*F*rom the Acts of Peter, the saint narrates a profound parable about a
sea voyage with the eleven apostles to an island city. There he meets
a pearl seller called Lithargoel. Following his instructions they prepare for
a journey to the City of Nine Gates. On arrival Lithargoel reveals himself
as Christ incognito, and talks with Peter, giving him further instructions.
The allegory probably dates from the second century.

With eleven apostles, I, Peter,
decided to attempt a sea voyage
in search of an unknown country,
as an adventure for our souls.
In our hearts we were all of one mind,
and covenanted to fulfil the ministry
to which our Lord, Jesus Christ had called us.

We went down to a port,
when we were prompted by God's will
and hired a fine ship, moored on the beach,
but all set to sail.
We talked with the sailors

about our coming aboard with them,
and they kindly agreed,
as obviously preordained by our Father.

After we embarked we sailed
for a whole day and one night,
a strong wind blew up
and swept us on to a small island city;
there were citizens standing on the quayside
and I asked them what was the name
of their attractive island home?

A spokesman among them replied saying
that the city was called "Habitation",
which I took to signify "foundation" and "endurance";
then this chief amongst them came to the dockside
waving a palm branch as a sign of welcome.

We disembarked with our baggage
and entered the strange city
to find somebody who would give us sound advice
about a good hostelry in which to stay.

We saw a man wearing a cloth cummerbund
tied by a golden belt;
a toga was slung loosely over his shoulders
yet covering his head and hands.

I gazed at this fine-looking figure intensely,
because he looked so noble
with such a strong build and commanding height;
I observed the soles of his feet, a glimpse of his chest,
and the palms of his hands, and compelling face.

He was holding a book with a leather cover in his left hand,
in his right, he held a well-crafted stick of styrax wood.
When he spoke, his voice was deep and sonorous,
Slowly he called out like a town crier,
"Pearls! Pearls! who wants Pearls?"

I believed him to be a citizen of the place,
and addressed him, saying,
"Hail! my dear brother and friend."
He quickly responded saying,
"You were quite right to call me your brother
and friend, what is it you require from me?"

I replied, "I would like you to please recommend
some good lodgings for our party,
because we're strangers to your fair city".

He answered, "That's why I, myself,
call you my brother and my friend,
because I am also a visitor here like your good selves!"
Then having spoke he again called out,

"Pearls! Pearls! who wants Pearls?"

Some wealthy traders heard his cry
and looked out of their warehouses,
others peered out of office windows,
but they didn't seem to think he was of real worth,
because he was without a pouch on his back,
and wasn't carrying a bundle of merchandise,
so they ignored him.

They talked with each other from their businesses
and agreed that this man was fooling them;
but the city's poor also heard his cry
and they tumbled out of their shacks and hovels
to see this man who sells pearls.

A crowd, almost with one voice, cried,
"Please be so kind as to show us a pearl,
that we may see one with our own eyes,
we're poor and we don't have any money to buy one,
but please show it to us,
so we can tell all of our friends
we have actually seen a precious pearl!"

The pearl seller said to them,
"If you possibly can, visit my own city
so that I may not only show you a real pearl,

but give you one for nothing!"

The poverty-stricken crowd heard his call
and cried, "As we're all beggars,
we know for sure that a merchant
doesn't hand over a pearl except for cash,
it's food and alms we mainly get, if at all!
The only favour we want from you,
is to show us the precious pearl
so we can see a real one and tell our pals!"

He shouted back at them,
"If you can, come to my city
so I can show it to you
and still give it to you for nothing!"
The mob cheered this good man,
willing to give them something for nothing!

Peter then asked the pearl seller his name,
and whether there were any difficulties
on the way to his city?
"As we're strangers and ministers of God,
it's needful that we spread His Word
in every possible place."

He replied, "My name is Lithargoel,
which means 'a stone, its light gleaming

like an eye of the gazelle!'
Now, about the route to my city,
no one is allowed to go that way
except those who've given up all that they own,
and have fasted each day from point to point.

"There are many thieves and wild brutes there,
anyone who carries bread with him,
black hounds will kill for food;
anyone who takes an expensive coat with him,
thieves will kill, to steal it;
anyone who carries a flask of fresh water,
is killed by thirsty wolves,
and anyone fearful about getting plenty of lamb
and green vegetables, the lions eat;
if he escapes the lions,
then bulls kill him for the green vegetables!"

When he'd said all this I groaned within myself,
thinking, great trials are on this path,
if only Christ would give me the power and
wisdom to walk on it!

Lithargoel gazed at me and said, "Why do you moan,
if you know the name Jesus and have faith in him?;
he's a mighty power for giving strength and courage;
I too believe in his Father who sent him!"

I asked him the name of his city.
He said, "It's known as the City of Nine Gates.
Give thanks to Almighty God so we remember the tenth!"

And then, somewhat cryptically
he said, "It's called the Self!"
Pondering somewhat on this strange name
I left him in peace.

As I proceeded to call my brother apostles
I saw huge waves, like high walls,
surrounding the city we were in;
I was astounded and seeing an elder on a bench
I asked him if this city's name
was really "Habitation"?

He answered, "Yes, we inhabit this place
because we endure!"
I replied and said, "It's a good name,
because through all who endure their trials,
cities are inhabited, and a good kingdom is born;
and they survive in spite of disasters
and terrible weather; so does the city of all
who endure their troubles sent to them in life.
With perfect faith they will be 'inhabited'
and one day ascend to heaven!"

I hurried to my fellow apostles
so we could prepare to go to Lithargoel's city;
in faithful agreement with his instructions
we renounced everything;
so we escaped the thieves and wild brutes
because we had nothing for them
to make them want to kill us.

Holy joy descended on us,
we felt absolutely carefree and at peace,
our whole burden of fear had
been handed over to God,
according to our Lord's command!

We relaxed before the gate and
talked about spiritual matters
which weren't worldly distractions,
and meditated in perfect faith!

Suddenly a nobleman, perhaps a physician, appeared.
He looked like a medical doctor, as he held an unguent box,
and a young follower was carrying a bag of medicines,
walking behind him; we didn't know who he was.

I said, "Please help us, we are travellers,
can you direct us to the house
of a certain pearl merchant called Lithargoel,

before sunset arrives?"

He replied, "In truth I will direct you,
but I am astounded that you know this good fellow,
for he doesn't give himself away just to anybody,
because in fact he's really a prince.
Rest a while, as I have to attend to a sick patient,
then I'll come back."

He soon returned; then he turned to me and said "Peter!"
I was afraid, for how did he ever know my name was Peter?!
I asked him, "How do you know my name?"

The Doctor answered and said,
"I want you to recall who gave you this name, Peter?"
I said it was given to me by no less a one
than Lord Jesus Christ, Son of the Living God!

The physician replied, "Then recognise
who I am, dear Peter! He undid his cloak,
the one Lithargoel had disguised himself in,
to hide himself from us,
and sure enough it was Christ himself!

We all prostrated and fell down on bended knees before him,
and worshipped him with songs of praise!
The Master raised his hand and told us to stand up.

We spoke with him humbly, with heads bowed, and said,
"Whatever you command, we shall do,
but grant us thy power!"

He then passed Peter the unguent box
and the bag of medicines and said,
"Go back to 'Habitation',
persevere in endurance and persistence,
instruct all who believe in my Name,
because I have endured all the trials of faith!
I shall reward you! Give to the poor
so they have the sustenance they need,
until I give them what is even better!
That which I said I would give them, for nothing!"

Peter said, "Oh Lord, you've taught us all
to renounce the world and worldliness,
by your command we've obeyed; we are, however,
concerned about our daily bread,
and how can we find what is needed to feed the poor."

Our Lord replied, "Peter, it's essential that you understand
that God's Wisdom is worth much more than all the gold,
silver, precious stones and riches of this world!
Take my bag of medicines with you
and heal all the sick of that city who have faith in my Name!"

Peter trembled, and was too frightened to speak;
he called over John and asked him to answer;
John said, "We are afraid to say many words,
before you, but it's you who orders us to practise this skill,
and we aren't trained as physicians,
how then can we cure sickness?"

The Lord answered him and said,
"You've spoken correctly John,
for I know the doctors of the world
only heal what belongs to this world,
but the Doctor of Souls heals the heart!
Help their bodies first so that they have faith in you,
then you can heal the sickness of their hearts.

"As for the rich, they who don't even
see fit to acknowledge me,
but who wallow in wealth and arrogance,
with such men as these, steer clear,
don't even dine in their mansions!
nor become their friends,
less their materialism infects you;
many Christians have curried favour with the rich,
because they are sinful too,
and set bad examples for others to sin!
But judge them righteously
so that your ministry and my name

261

will be honoured and my Church glorified!"

The apostles answered, "Yes! we shall obey you!"
they prostrated before him;
he commanded them to rise and depart in peace!

Amen

JAMES'S HIDDEN BOOK

According to Gnostic tradition, James was Christ's actual blood brother. In this powerful tract he writes, for a Gnostic teacher, possibly Cerinthus, a secret book, meant for only a chosen few. Salvation is assured to all those who read it. This "Apocryphon" claims to be a hidden record of Jesus's ultimate teaching, when he reappears after The Resurrection. It is mainly in the form of dialogue, and was originally composed in Hebrew, but later translated both into Greek and Coptic. It is thought to date before AD 150.

My dear Reader, may peace, love, grace, faith
and the truly religious life be always with you!
as you sincerely enquired, I am sending you a hidden work,
which was revealed to Peter and I, by my own brother, Christ.

I couldn't refuse your earnest request,
so I'm sending this book to you alone,
as you minister for the salvation of saints;
but please take very special care
not to show the content to many,
as our Saviour kept it secret even from some of his disciples;
blessed are all those who're saved through this sacred work.

Early last year I sent you a different,
hidden book which Christ showed to me,
but this one was for the "Twelve" who were sitting together
recalling his words and writing them down;
when all of a sudden our Lord and Saviour appeared!
We gazed at him in awe,
as it was eighteen months since his resurrection!

We said to him, as if to a man, in fear and trembling,
"Have you left us completely?"
Jesus answered, "No!, but I'll return
to the place from where I came,
if you wish to come with me, then come!
We replied, "If you command us, then we shall come!"

He then said, "No one can enter the kingdom of heaven,
merely at my command,
but only if you are prepared and ready!
James and Peter be alone with me, so I may prepare them!"
He drew us aside and told the rest to leave us alone.

Jesus said to us, "You've received grace,
don't you wish to be properly prepared?
Your hearts are intoxicated with worldliness,
don't you wish to be sobered up?
Be shamed! awake, or asleep,
try to recall that you've seen the Son of Man

and talked with him personally
and paid attention to his words!

"You'll inherit eternal life,
he healed you when you were sick,
that you might rule over yourselves!;
grief to those who've only found relief from sickness
for they will fall for sick again;
blessed are those who've never been sick,
theirs is the kingdom of heaven!

"So I command you to come, well prepared,
leave no room within you unfulfilled,
or he who is coming may scorn you!"

Peter said, "Master, three times you've told us
to become fulfilled, but we are fulfilled!"
Jesus answered, "I've asked you to be fulfilled
so you won't be lacking in remembering your Divine Self,
as they'll not be saved who forget.

Paradoxically it's good to be in want,
so as to be fulfilled more often,
and not forget your Divine Self so much;
so become full of Spirit, but be lacking in reason,
as rationality belongs to the mind,
an offshoot of the soul, not the Self."

I responded and said, "Lord we shall obey you
if you order us, for we've detached from our parents
and towns to follow you.
Guard us that we shan't be led astray
by that devilish, wicked, adverse one!"

Jesus replied, "Where's the virtue
if you obey God's will, and grace isn't given
while you're tempted by your enemy, Satan;
but if you're harrassed by your foe,
and you obey your Father's will,
I say He'll love you and make you the same as I am!

So reflect that you've become beloved
through His grace, and your own free will!
So please cease adoring your bodily desires
and being frightened of suffering!
Don't you know that in due time
you'll be persecuted, falsely charged, gaoled,
condemned illegally, crucified without reason,
and entombed in disgrace,
as I was, my Self, by Satanic powers!

So risk to end fleshly impulses,
you for whom your Spirit is still an encompassing wall;
if you reflect on the age of the world before you existed,
and how long it will go on after you've gone,

you'll find your life is but one day, in eternity,
and your suffering lasted only an hour!

The Good will not re-enter the world,
so mock death with the deathless Self,
and reflect on life everlasting!
Remember the emblem of my Cross
and my crucifixion, and you shall live!"

I said, "Lord, don't recall your Cross and death,
they are now distant from you!"
Jesus replied, "I am telling you the truth when I say
that none of you'll be saved
unless you believe in the emblem of my Cross,
but for those who have great faith,
they shall know the Kingdom of God!
So become seekers for the death of the egotistic petty self,
like the dead who seek for life,
for that which they seek shall be found!

And there'll be nothing left to frighten or disturb them again;
when you scrutinise death, and enquire 'who dies?'
it'll show you the way to be chosen.
So none who fear this death of self will be saved,
for God's Kingdom belongs to those who commit egocide!
Be more perfect than I,
transform yourselves as children of the Holy Spirit!"

Then I asked, "How shall we prophesy
to those who ask us to prophesy?; there are many
who expect to hear something oracular from us!"
He replied, "Don't you know that the head of prophecy
was decapitated with the Baptist!"

I asked how this was possible?
He said, "When you know the true meaning of 'head'
and the prophesy issues from the 'head',
you'll understand the significance of 'its head was cut off'.

At first I taught you with parables, and you failed to hear,
now I speak directly and you still don't see,
yet it was you who served me as a living parable in my parables,
and as that is revealed in the words that are revealed!

Hurry, be saved without being kicked!
Be earnest and sincere, and try to get there before me
then my Father will love you!
Despise hypocrisy and impure thought,
for thought is the mother of the hypocrites
and they are very distant from truth!

Don't allow the kingdom of heaven
to rot like the autumn rose
or like the palm shoot whose fruit has fallen!;
the fallen fruit shoots leaves

and after sprouting the plant dries up.
For those with ears to hear, let them hear!

Since I've already been glorified,
why do you keep me here, when I'm keen to leave?
You've made me stay here for two and a half weeks
to teach with more parables;
it was enough for some to hear my teaching
and immediately comprehend.

Become sincere and zealous about the Word;
it's first, great faith, secondly, unconditional love,
thirdly, devoted works, from these,
the fountain of life flows freely and forever!

The Word is like a golden grain of harvest wheat,
the farmer who sowed it had faith in its power to grow,
and when it flourished, he loved it,
because now there were many grains instead of just one;
after his work he was nourished,
because he baked it as bread, and again he left some to sow.

So you too can receive the kingdom of heaven;
unless you accept this complete Self knowledge
you won't be able to find it.
So I say 'sober up'! don't be misled!
and many times I've addressed you all,

and to you alone, my dear brother James,
have I implored 'be saved!'
and I've ordered you to follow my example,
and I've told you what to say to the archons.

See that I've come down, spoke, and undergone suffering,
and carried off my crown of thorns after saving you both.
I came down to live with you so that you might live with me,
And finding your houses not hermetically sealed,
I have made my home in the houses of those
who welcomed me when I came down.

So trust me, my brothers,
experience what the Great Primal Light really is.
My Father doesn't require me, He doesn't need a son,
but the son needs a father, so I go to Him!
The Father of the Son hasn't a need for you.

"Listen to the Word, comprehend Self knowledge,
love true life, no one shall revile you, nor harrass you,
other than your own petty egotistic self!
Oh, you poor fools, idiots mimics of the truth,
falsifiers of my doctrine, sinners against the spirit,
can you still bear to listen
when it's proper you speak from the Primal Self?

Can you stand to be sunk in deep hypnotic sleep

when you should be wide awake
so the kingdom of Heaven might receive you?
I say it's easier for a pure man to fall into degradation,
than for a man of light to fall into darkness,
as it's hard for you to rule yourself
or easy not to rule over yourself.

I have recalled your grief while you say
'the people are far behind us',
but now you're outside your Father's heritage,
so cry where necessary, and preach what is Good,
as the Son of Man is ascending as he should ascend.

Had I been sent just for those able to listen to me,
I wouldn't have come down to this world!
So be ashamed of all these shortcomings,
as soon I shall leave; I don't want to stay with you any more,
for you have not really wanted me.

It's better to follow me speedily, for your sakes,
I descended, you're the beloved, you're the ones
who'll be the source of new life for many people!
Pray to the Father often and he'll grant you His grace;
Blest am I, the Son, who saw you with my Father
when I was glorified amongst the angels
and proclaimed amongst the saints.

Yours is the life everlasting!
celebrate and be happy as children of the Father!
Obey His will that you may find salvation;
receive rebukes from me, so you may save yourselves!
I shall intervene on your behalf with my Father
and He shall forgive you!"

When Peter and I heard these words, we rejoiced heartily!
for we had been troubled by the words
the Lord uttered before;
but when he saw us celebrating he said to us,
"Beware all those in need of an intercessor with my Father,
and require His grace!
Blest will they be who have called out and obtained His grace!

Compare yourselves with aliens,
what kind of men are they in the sight of your village?
Why are you troubled?; free yourselves from your village.
Why don't you leave of your own free will
making room for those who wish to live there?

Oh strangers, and refugees, beware or you'll be trapped!
Do you imagine that your Father
is a lover of unregenerate humanity?;
or that He is convinced without heartfelt prayer?;
or that He gives forgiveness to you on someone else's behalf?;
or that He forbears one who merely asks?

For he sees desire and what the flesh craves!
This flesh desires to own your soul,
for without the soul's agreement the body won't sin,
the soul will not be saved without the cooperation of the spirit,
but if the soul's saved when it's purified, along with the spirit,
then your body will be sinless!

It's the spirit that lifts the soul
and the flesh which tries to kill it!
So, in effect, the unwilling soul commits suicide!
The Father won't pardon that sin, nor the flesh its shame,
for none of those with carnal intent will be saved;
do you imagine many have found God's kingdom?!"

When we heard this warning we were troubled;
but when our Lord saw our tribulation he said,
"I tell you all this, so as to impel both of you
to try to know your own Divine Self!

For the kingdom is again like an ear of golden grain
after growing in a field;
when it matures, it sheds its seed,
replenishes the field with ears of golden wheat
for yet another glorious harvest!
So hurry and reap an ear of eternal life for yourselves
that you may be fulfilled in the kingdom of heaven!

So as long as I am with you, listen to me
and follow my instruction, and when I leave,
remember me because when I was among you both,
you failed to realise who I truly am!
Blest will all those be who know me as I really am,
beware those who've listened but have little faith!;
even more blest are those who haven't seen,
yet have great faith!

Once more I implore you, for I come to you,
building a mansion of great worth
when you take shelter beneath its roof;
it will stand firm by your neighbour's house,
when it looks like falling down;
beware! all those for whose sake I descended to this world,
blest will be those who ascend to my Father's mansion.

Once again I urge you all who've become
like those who are full of petty self,
to become like those who are nullified,
so you may dwell with them.

Don't turn God's kingdom into an arid desert within yourself;
don't boast, because of the primal light that illuminates all,
but be true to your own Self as I my Self am to you!
For your sakes I have placed myself under tribulation
that you may be saved!"

Peter responded to these noble words and said,
"Sometimes you impel us on to the kingdom,
and then you seem to turn us back;
sometimes you move us to great faith
and promise us eternal life, and then
you seem to throw us out of heaven, why?"

Jesus answered, "I've filled you with great faith
many times, and visited you after my resurrection,
yet both you Peter, and my brother James, have,
up to now, failed to recognise who I really, really am!

I see you both celebrating
when you're promised everlasting life,
but you grieve when you're instructed
about how to reach the kingdom;
yet through faith and knowledge
you've received everlasting life,
so don't reject it when you learn more about it,
but celebrate more!

He who will accept eternal life
and have faith in the kingdom will never leave it,
not even if my Father decides to expel him!
This is all I intend to tell you so far before I re-ascend
to the place from which I descended;
but you, when I was keen to go, rejected the idea,

and instead of coming with me,
you have chased me for knowledge.

So listen to the splendour that waits for me,
and having opened up your heart,
listen to the hymns of praise
that will greet my arrival in heaven.

Today I must resume my seat at the right hand of my father;
this is my final message to you both before I leave;
a chariot of spirit has lifted me on high,
and now I shall disrobe myself of this body
so I may clothe myself in an ethereal robe.

Take notice, blest are those who declared the Son of Man
before he came down to the world!
so when I descended, I might re-ascend;
three times blest are those declared by the Son of Man
before they even existed, so that you may rejoice
in a share of these immortal souls for greater good."

Having spoken these fine words he ascended up to heaven,
and we both prostrated with gratitude,
lifting up our hearts heavenward;
we heard in our ears, and saw in a vision, the tumult of war,
a trumpet's call, and a great furore!

When we had both left that scene,
we lifted our hearts and souls further upwards
and saw and heard angelic hosts
chanting melodious hymns of praise,
and we too rejoiced with them;
again we wished to lift our spirits to the King of Kings,
our Father in Heaven.

And after our ascent we were not permitted to see
or hear any visions as other disciples interrupted us
and asked, "What did the Lord say, and where has he gone?"

We told them, "He's ascended and given us
his promise of everlasting life, to us all,
and showed us his children who shall succeed us,
after telling us to love them,
as we would be saved for their sakes!"

When the disciples heard this they believed our revelation
but were unhappy about those to be born;
but not wishing to dispute I sent them away,
and I went up to Jerusalem to pray that I might share
a portion among the beloved who would follow us;

I pray that this rebirth may issue from you, dear reader,
for then I'll be fit for salvation
since you shall be enlightened through me,

by my great faith, and through the Son's faith,
which is even greater than mine!

Work zealously to make yourself like them
and pray that you too, may share a portion
with these preordained, pure souls.
Our Saviour didn't reveal all this teaching
for their sakes alone; we too claim a share
with those for whom this proclamation was made!
and all those whom our gracious Lord Jesus Christ
has made his children!
Amen.

THE SEXTUS PROVERBS

The pithy aphorisms of Sextus were known, before the Nag Hammadi discovery, from two ancient Greek manuscripts. These wise sayings were very popular in Christian circles, and probably derive from the early first-century Egyptian Monastic Orders. They are generally included in the Gnostic Literature because of their date and stringent ascetism.

Adore truth and hate lies,
like a viper's venom.

Pray that an auspicious moment
will dawn before you speak.

Hold silence when speech is uncalled for,
and only speak about what you've actually experienced!

The untimely, hurtful, uncalled for phrase
points to an impure mind.

When right action is needed,
refrain from foolish verbiage!

Don't wish to be the first
to advise the mob.

Eloquence is a skill,
but to keep silent is much more skilful.

It's better to be beaten up telling the truth
than to be triumphant, telling lies!

A victor in deceit
will be vanquished by the truth.

Lying statements indicate
a pernicious individual.

A major catastrophe is needed
before any deceit becomes necessary.

Never deceive anyone
who comes for your advice!

If you're the last to speak,
you'll see what's worthwhile, more clearly.

To be first in executing good deeds,
is a sign of fidelity.

Divine wisdom lifts the pure soul
to the kingdom of heaven.

Truth hasn't any near relative,
except for wisdom.

It's impossible for a faithful soul
to enjoy telling lies.

A fearful, slavish nature
won't benefit from the power of Faith.

If you're wise, then what's good to say,
isn't always better than just listening.

When you're with a man of Faith,
it's better to listen than to spout opinion.

A man who only loves pleasure
is pretty well useless.

When your faults aren't self-observed,
don't burble on about God.

The sins of the ignorant
are the everlasting shame of their teachers.

Blasphemers are spiritually dead,
in the sight of God.

A Sage does all his deeds
in God's Name.

May your deeds confirm your words
to your listeners.

Never, ever, contemplate
doing anything that's wrong!

What you wouldn't want to happen to you,
don't do to yourself!

He's a Sage who recommends God to Man.

God thinks more highly of the Sage
than of His own work.

After God Himself, nobody's as free as a Sage.

All that God owns,
is owned by the Master of Self Knowledge!

The Sage, who knows his own Divine Selfhood,
dwells in God's Kingdom.

An ignoramus fears
that God's Will may happen to him.

A malevolent Soul flies away
from his Lord and Master.

Evil is God's Demonic adversary.

Where your thoughts are,
so dwells your goodness.

Don't search for goodness
in your prurient body of flesh.

He who doesn't hurt his own Soul
won't hurt another's.

After God, respect the Sage,
for he's God's servant.

To make your Soul's chariot, the body,
a burden on your head, is foolish and arrogant
but to rein in its impetuous steeds gently, is grace.

Don't commit spiritual suicide.

Don't rage against God,
who'll release you from your vile body,
and slay your egotism!

If someone kills a Sage wickedly
he does what's best for him,
he's freed him from the prison of this world
and the cycle of continuous rebirth.

Fear of approaching death terrifies man,
because of his inherent ignorance!

Someone who feigns belief
will not prevail, he'll topple!

As your Being is,
so your life will be.

A heart devoted to God
assures a carefree life!

He who plots evil against another
is the first to suffer from a murderous conspiracy!

Don't let an ungrateful recipient

stop you from performing good deeds.

Never think that anything which was begged for,
and you gave it immediately,
is more worthy than the beggar himself!

You use possessions wisely
if you give to the poor willingly!

Train a crazy brother not to act crazily,
if he's really crazy, guard him.

Try earnestly to win over everybody else in "prudence",
this protects your self-sufficiency!

You'll never gain understanding,
unless you first possess a grain of it,
this applies to pretty well anything and everything.

The body's functions will become problematic for those
who don't make good use of them, but abuse them.

It's far better to wait on others,
than have others wait upon you.

Don't hold views which fail to help the needy,
and don't listen to those that do.

Whoever gives a gift without due reverence
commits an offence.

If you foster an orphan, you'll be father for a needy child,
and be blessed by God.

If you serve someone just to win fame,
it's the same as being hired for a fee.

If you work to win fame,
you haven't worked to help your fellow man,
but for your own self-aggrandizement.

Never provoke the wrath of a crowd,
but know what's right for a fortunate man to do.

It's better to die than pollute your soul
by overindulgence.

Remember your body is the soul's temporary robe,
keep it pure and innocent.

Whatever sin the soul does, in the flesh,
will testify on judgement day.

Dirty spirits cling to a dirty soul,
but they can't hurt a soul devoted to God.

Don't preach God's Word to anyone,
without due discrimination.

For those corrupted by vanity,
it's disturbing to hear about God!

It's unwise to talk about God
before you've known Him directly.

Never talk with the Godless about God.

If you're corrupted by impure deeds,
don't discuss God.

The Truth about God
is in His Word.

Speak about the Word of God
as if in His Presence.

Only if you're truly devoted to God
should you speak about Him.

May deeds of devotion always precede
your words about God.

Never speak to the mob about God!

Be more sparing in your words about God,
than about your own soul.

You may see the form of the God-loving Sage,
but you can't command his speech!

If a tyrant threatens you,
then remember your Divine Self.

It's better to keep silent about the Almighty
than talk from ignorance.

It's impossible to know God unless you worship Him,
and know your own Divine Self which is also God.

Anyone who deliberately harms another
won't be able to worship God.

Love for your fellow man
is the first step in Godliness.

It's God's choice to save whom he wishes to save;
it's the task of the man of God to pray that he'll save
everyone.

A man Self Realised by God,
is a God among men, and a son of God.

It's better to be without anything
than to have too much of everything
while not giving charity to the poor.

If from your whole heart you give to the needy,
the gift may be small,
but your willingness is great in God's sight.

He who doesn't believe that all are in the presence of God
and the Self, lacks humility.

It's the man of faith who's fond of learning
who is the developer of truth.

Even a cruel tyrant
can't rob you of inner happiness.

Whatever good you do well,
say that it's God who does it.

The philosopher who lives mainly in the external world,
is not the one to respect,
but the Sage who lives inwardly in God,
is worthy of reverence.

Realise your own True Self
and you'll know who God is.

ALLOGENES

Allogenes or The Foreigner, has a great revelation and recounts it to his son Messos. In this second part, he educates him on how to regard each stage of the path to the full Realisation of one's own Divine Self. The Greek text has Gnostic Mystical and Platonic influences and was known to have been in Alexandria, somewhere before AD 270 as the work was known to Plotinus.

Oh Messos, my dearest son,
I never despaired from the teachings I've heard,
I've meditated on them for a century;
inspired, I constantly prepared and refreshed myself,
to march on in my mighty quest!

Then the grace of everlasting hope descended,
filled with unconditional love, I saw the benevolent,
Godlike, Self-originated aeon, the Messiah,
the triply masculine perfected child,
his essentially benevolent nature,
the ideal Harmedon, the original intellectual power,
the holiness of the hidden aeon,
the primal source of grace, the Barbelo,
filled with Godliness, infinite, threefold,

unseen omnipotent spirit,
the whole, more perfect than the perfect!

After being dazzled and enveloped
by everlasting primordial light,
emanating from the sacred robe
that I had ceremonially donned,
and taking up a pose for contemplation
and silence, in a sacred place,
that bore not the slightest relationship
without our solely troubled world,
I witnessed all the splendid visions,
about which I had been informed,
and I praised all of them, and stood still,
at perfect ease, with my Self.

I turned within towards gnostic recognition
of the whole of the Barbelo aeon,
and saw sacred forces from the great lights
of the androgynous Barbelo,
which intimated that I should try to remain in this world
of tears and sorrow.
"Oh Allogenes, see how your gracious Self
dwells in a plentitude of silence
through which you come to know your true Self
as you really, really are!
And in searching to know your true Self more widely,

withdraw the vital urge, which you'll see as serpentine,
ascending in a spiralling upward motion.

If you're ever prevented from resting in stillness,
never feel a hint of fear.
Withdraw from the senses and turn inwards
to the Real which dwells within you,
at the still, silent centre which constrains spiritual beings
from ceaseless activity, and if, in that zone,
you reach the sphere of perfection, remain completely still.

If you receive a manifestation
which is totally unknown and unrecognisable,
and are overawed there,
because of the seeming movement,
withdraw your senses, be perfectly still,
and know this all reflects
the unborn image of God within you;
don't become fragmented so you may rest at peace,
deep inside your heart,
and have no wish to resume mental activity
or you'll destroy this blessed state.

Don't try to comprehend this miracle
of Self Remembering and Self Abidance,
it's well beyond any explanation by the mind,
thought, reason, or language!"

Then I felt the presence
of the ineffable unknowable One,
the great invisible spirit,
more perfect than the perfect,
a primal manifestation
with the triply powered silence,
that exists in all beings,
found in stillness and quietness
and is not cognisable.

When I became firm in this place,
the voices of the great Primordial Lights
spoke to me and said,
"It's possible that through seeking the unknowable,
you might fragment the passive element
that dwells in you, yet pay attention
for it's most probable with a primary manifestation;
the fundamental question arises,
as to whether this Unknowable One,
the uncognisable can be cognised?

For it's not exactly pure Godliness,
Grace, nor Flawlessness;
rather each of these is an uncognisable
inessential quality of 'That',
and not its fundamental quiddity.

"It seems to be something 'other', a superior power,
it's neither boundless nor are boundaries imposed upon it,
it cannot be described as embodied or bodiless,
it isn't vast nor minute, quantifiable nor unquantifiable,
neither a creature nor an existent,
it's something greater than all this
beyond one's comprehension.

'That' is a primary manifestation,
prior to all other manifestations,
original and Self originated,
it's best described as the Supreme
amongst the Supremest!
it neither shares in timelessness
nor in passages of passing spasms of time,
it neither receives from another
nor bestows anything on another,
nor is it anything, nor is it nothing.

In terms of the 'beautiful' it's sublime,
and far superior to all
that's commonly termed 'good';
so it's utterly and completely uncognisable
to anyone or by anyone,
although it permeates 'all'
it cannot be termed 'all',
it is indescribable, ineffable,

neither 'this' nor 'that',
the essential what-isness,
beyond the knowable!

"Sublime, still, silent, quiet,
inscrutable, its own Self alone,
unborn, deathless Reality;
'That' doesn't activate nor non-activate anything,
not even its own Self,
and has no will or determination,
neither omnipotent nor impotent,
a spiritless habitation,
it accepts all in its stillness,
peaceful in that which ever stands utterly at peace.

This Triply Powered, Great Unknown,
Incognisable, Invisible Spirit – the One,
which is in All, envelops All, permeates All
although being more exalted than All.
It rests in peace prior to All,
bestowing power upon All and fulfilling All!"

This is the summation of that
which is beyond understanding
and cognition, my son!

So dear Messos, you've paid attention well,

and heard all these secret revelations;
don't try to comprehend
the incomprehensible any further,
nor whether the silence
has anything in it other than silence,
that is its own Absolute Divine Self!
We aren't angels,
nor is it good to become fragmented
by trying to know the unknowable.

That Power said to me, "Copy down
whatever I tell you for posterity,
and place the book on a mountain
and call upon Phriktos, custodian of Death!"
Filled with holy joy, I wrote the book as commanded;
oh Messos, this is what was shown to me in that Silence.

Amen

THOMAS
THE CONTENDER

This novel Coptic tract is an admonitory dialogue between the resurrected Jesus and a supposed "twin brother" called Judas Thomas, just before Christ's Ascension. This "twin relationship" may perhaps be interpreted as meaning you, your Self, as a devoted Christian. It is told by Mathaias, possibly St Matthew. It probably dates from around the third century AD, translated from a missing Greek text.

These are the hidden words
that our Lord and Saviour, Jesus Christ,
told to his Disciple, Judas Thomas.

I, Mathaias, noted it all down
while walking, listening, or talking with them.

Christ said, "Brother Thomas,
while you still have time on Earth,
pay attention to what I say, and I'll tell you
all that you've wondered about in your mind.

Now since it's been said that you're my twin

and true companion, enquire within yourself
and discover who you really, really are!

Find out in what way you actually exist,
and how you came to be.
Since you're called my brother it's not right
for you to be ignorant of your true nature.

I know you've accepted that
I am the knowledge of the Truth!
So while we're together,
although you lack understanding,
you have in a way, come to see,
and may be termed
one who's had a glimpse
of his Real Self.

He who doesn't know his own Self
knows virtually nothing,
but he who does, has gained knowledge
of the profundity of the 'All'.

So dear Brother Thomas, you've seen what's hard
and perplexing for mankind to understand,
and what they trip up against, in their spiritual blindness."

Thomas spoke to our Lord,

"Pray, tell me what I ask before your Ascension,
so when I learn about these secrets, I may speak about them,
as it's clear that it's hard to live the truth before men."

Christ replied, "If the seen's unclear to you,
how can you be clear about the unseen?
If acts of truth are hard to perform,
how can you expect to reach exalted peaks
and the Pleroma which are unseen?

How can you be called craftsmen?
In this way, you're apprentices,
who haven't yet reached
the pinnacle of perfection!"

Thomas answered,
"Then please tell us about these mysteries
concealed from our sight."

Christ said, "Each body, even of beasts,
when they're born, are animated
by the life force which emanates from above,
it's obvious and can be seen.

This is their root, and nature's fruits should feed them;
but these beasts also live by eating beasts like themselves
so their bodies go through change.

"Now that which changes, decays and dies,
and loses spiritual hope,
as the body has now become bestial.
So just as bestial bodies die, so will their subtle forms;
men and women are born
from carnal intercourse like animals.

So if the body comes from intercourse
how will it breed anything different from animality?
So you're spiritual novices
until you become whole and flawless."

Thomas said, "In my view, those that talk
about things unseen which are hard to understand
are like those who fire arrows
at a target in the night!

Yes, they fire arrows all right, but the target isn't seen.
Yet when dawn breaks then their aim can be noted,
and you're that Light to enlighten us, oh Lord!"

Jesus replied, "Yes, it's in the Light that the Light lives!"
Thomas asked, "Why does the ordinary light
that shines for people, rise and set?"

Jesus answered, "Of course, this visible light
shines for you all, not for you to wait here,

but for you to move on.

When all the Chosen Ones renounce animality,
then this light will return to its source
which will welcome it gladly, as it's a faithful servant!

Oh inscrutable passion of the light,
fierce is the fire that blazes in human flesh
and in their bones, intoxicating and destabilising
their souls and minds.

There's too much cohabitation
between men and women;
lust moves them covertly and openly,
the male assails the female
and the female assails the male.

So those who seek the Truth from wisdom
must themselves create wings
and fly from that fire which singes the soul of man,
and flee from every spiritual disease."

Thomas said, "Lord, this is exactly
what I'm enquiring about
since I now know that you're the One
who's of real help to man!"

Christ replied, "It's essential that I speak with you
as this is the perfect teaching for the flawless;
if you yearn earnestly to become flawless
you'll keep these doctrines.

If not, then your name's 'Ignorant One'
as it's impossible for an enlightened soul to talk with a fool,
for the Enlightened is perfect in spiritual wisdom.

For the foolish, good and evil are confused,
and often no distinction is made;
the wise Sage is fed by Truth.

As David sang in his first Psalm,
'He'll be like a tree planted by streams of water,
that bears fruit in due season,
and whose leaves never fade;
and in whatever he tries, he'll triumph.'

There are some who seem to have created
wings of aspiration yet still desire visible attractions
that are a long way from the Truth.

For that false fire which leads them
will give only a semblance of truth,
and will shine on them with a glow that will wane,
and bind them in excessive comfort

and entrap them in seductive hedonism.

It'll blind their spiritual sight with insatiable lust
and scorch their souls like a stake,
stuck in the heart, which they can't remove,
or be like a horse's bit,
which dashes wildly to feed on selfish desires.

It's chained their bodies
with the agony of lust for tangible pleasure,
moved by impulse, that'll wither and die.
They are drawn down as they are slain,
where they join the beasts of the perishable domain."

Thomas answered, "It's obvious, and as you've said,
'Many are called but few are chosen,'
and don't know their own Self."

Jesus said, "Blessed is the wise man or woman
who seeks earnestly after truth, and when he finds, he rests,
and is never afraid again of anything sent to upset him."

Thomas asked, "Is it good for us to rest among our own?"
Christ replied, "Yes, it's worthwhile; it's beneficial,
since sensual attractions among you will dissipate.

The fleshly container will dissolve,

and when it's rendered to nothing,
they'll return to the world of visibility,
and their inner fire will feel painful
because of the loss of faith they suffered.

For those who have insight into that which is unseen,
but without their first love of strong faith,
they'll perish in anxiety about this life,
and lust will stay as their burning fire.

A little time more,
and even the perceivable will dissipate,
and ghosts will emerge from the middle of graveyards
and eat corpses in the pain and suffering of their souls!"

Thomas said, "What can we say in the face of all that?
What can we say to the spiritually blind?
What teaching should we give to these afflicted souls
who claim 'we came to do good and not to curse'
and yet boast 'if we hadn't been born into flesh
we wouldn't have known any sin?'"

Christ said, "Don't even respect them as human beings,
but regard them as animals, for as beasts eat one another
so men of this type swallow each other up.

They're barred from the Kingdom,

as they worship the sweet meats of fiery lust
and are slaves of death, hastening to perdition!

They fulfil the cravings of their ancestors,
they'll be cast down to the pit and suffer
from the pain of shame, by their wickedness.

They'll be purged to make them turn inwards,
to where they don't know, and they'll part
from their bodily identification with distress.

They chase this insanity obliviously
even imagining they're wise!
Their minds are focused on their own egotism
and their thoughts full of 'doing this and that',
but the fire of lust will consume them!"

Thomas replied, "Lord what should anyone sent to them do?
I'm concerned about them, as many folk oppose them."
Jesus answered, "What's your own view on this matter?"

Judas Thomas said, "It's for you to speak master,
and for me to attend!"

Christ answered, "Pay attention!
and have faith in my truth,
that which sows and what is sown

will be consumed in the fire of their carnal appetites,
and within the fire, and the water,
they will lurk in darkest graves.

After some while the fruit of their wickedness
will be punished, they'll be killed by beasts or men.
All will be made to happen by the forces of nature,
the rains, the gales, the air and the light, radiant above."

Thomas said, "You've convinced us,
we see your truth in our hearts,
and it is obviously the case,
your word is adequate authority.

But to the world your words
will sound absurd and unacceptable
since they are misconstrued,
so how can we preach since we're scorned?"

Christ answered, "I tell you that
whoever listens to your word and scornfully denies,
will be delivered to the King of Kings
and he will turn that soul about
and cast him from heaven into the pit,
captive, in a shallow dark world.

He will be unable to turn within or move outwards

because of deep Tartaros
and the weight of Hades that's established,
and they'll be given to the angel Tartarouchos
and be chased by fire.

Fire purges and flings sparks
into the face of the one who's chased.
North, South, and West he meets this scourge.
Only in the East will he find refuge
but he's lost his way there,
as he did not seek it in the flesh
so he could find it on judgement day.

Sorrow to all Godless ones who are hopeless,
and trust that which is impossible;
sorrow to all who trust in the flesh
and the jail of a world which will die.

How long will you remain ignorant?
How long will you think that the undying will die also?
Your faith is fixed upon the world;
your god is the material life, your souls are contaminated!

Sorrow to all, burning within the fire
that scorches, it's ravenous!
Sorrow to you because of the constant wheel of thought
that revolves in your minds.

Sorrow to all, singed by the lustful fire within,
it will eat up your substance, secretly tear your soul
and prepare you for death with your comrades.

Sorrow to all prisoners, bound in caves,
you celebrate with insane laughter,
you're unaware of your spiritual condition
and fail to scrutinise your situation.

You fail to comprehend that you dwell
in spiritual darkness and death,
you're intoxicated with the fires of lust
and full of sourness; your brain is deranged
because of this inward burning,
you even find the poison and blows
of your foes to be sweet!

Darkness rose for you as if it was light,
you renounced your freedom for slavery,
ransomed your thoughts to foolish imagination,
and the smoke of that lustful fire within,
which burnishes your hearts.

Your pure light is veiled and your clothes are spotted,
caught by a hope that is nonexistent;
who is it you actually believe?
You mingle with mockers and scoffers,

you baptise your soul in dirty water,
you plod on, driven by your own fancies.

Sorrow to all who live in falsehood,
unaware that the Sun, which sees and judges,
will circle in orbit and capture His foes;
you don't even see how the moon gazes
at the victims of your murder!

Sorrow to all who worship
polluted intercourse with women,
in the grasp of flesh,
this will sooner or later be punished;
sorrow to all who are in the power
of evil spirits and devilish tendencies.

Who will comfort you
with the grace of refreshing morning dew
to snuff out your burning fires of lust?
Who will make the Sun of grace shine upon you
to disperse darkness in you
and dissolve the soul's polluted water?

Sun and moon will spray sweet perfume on you
together with the holy spirit, fresh air,
good earth and pure water.

If the Sun fails to shine upon bodies
they'll decay and die!
like the weeds of the field
and grass of the meadow.

If the sun shines on tares they triumph
and throttle vines; the sprouting scrub strangles the soil
on which they grow; but if the vine prevails
and shades the tares and weeds from sunlight,
they perish, and it pleases the farmer,
for he would have suffered great labour to uproot the weeds
which the vine effortlessly achieved.

Sorrow to all who fail to learn this teaching,
for those who're lost will struggle
by preaching and rushing into confusion;
this will bring them down; but you slay them daily,
so they might rise up from the dead!

Great blessings on all who have now learned
about the pitfalls and obstacles,
and will flee from corruption;
blessed are all who are demeaned and insulted
because of the love their Lord has bestowed upon them.

Blessed are all who shed tears and
are tormented by the hopeless,

for you'll be freed from all servitude.
Be vigilant! and pray you aren't snared by the flesh
and are freed from the jail of this worldly life.

As you worship you'll discover peace,
for you've renounced the pain of sin and guilt.

When you leave the desire and torment of the flesh
you'll receive peace from your God
and reign with your King,
you linked with Him and He with you
from now, and for all eternity!"

Amen

A PRAYER OF
SAINT PAUL

Many Gnostics saw Saint Paul as the founder of their lineage. This prayer, attributed to him, expresses Gnostic theology and the soul's yearning for salvation.

Redeem me, I AM is yours,
from you I've emerged.

It's you who are my mind, regenerate me.
It is you who are my treasure, grant some to me.

It's you who are my perfection, accept me
It is you who are my rest, give me expansive fullness.

I pray to you, oh existence, prior to any existence,
in the name, above every name, of Jesus Christ,
Lord of Lords, King of the Everlasting Kingdom.

Grant me your merciful gifts
through the innocent child inherent in the human
by grace of the holy Spirit, intermediary of truth.

Make me masterly I implore you, cure my bodily ailments,
I appeal as a teacher of your Gospel.

Ransom my illuminated soul for eternity and my Spirit.
Reveal to my mind the original perfection of your grace.

Show me what eyes of angels haven't yet seen,
what ears of emperors, haven't yet heard,
what hasn't yet visited the hearts of men and women,
who have become angelic! after the emblem of the living God
when he was formed at the genesis,
for I've great faith possessed by hope.

Grant me too, your Beloved elected, blessed Sovereignty
oh Self-originated primal creator
of the marvellous mystery of your mansion.

For yours is the Kingdom, the glory, the worship,
and the magnificence for ever and ever,
Amen

THE RESURRECTION

This short didactic Tract looks at the question of the afterlife and the resurrection of the dead. Esoterically, Christ often referred to the spiritually dead, and it is their spiritual resurrection or "raising up from the dead", as in the tale of Lazarus, which has most metaphorical relevance. This is a dialogue between an anonymous Christian Gnostic adept and his pupil Rheginos. The Teaching given is influenced by Valentinus and was probably composed before AD 350. The original Greek tract is missing and the surviving text is in Coptic.

There are many, my dear Rheginos,
who wish to learn a great deal,
they have this desire when their minds are bothered
by questions which they can't answer.

If they are successful they pat themselves on the back
but I don't believe they have actually experienced
the "Word" or "Logos of Truth".
They seek peace of mind which we've gained from Jesus.

But as you enquire about the resurrection,
I'm speaking with you.
It's necessary to be certain,
many lack faith in this teaching,

only a few find it, so we'll talk it over, my son.

How did our Lord teach when he was alive,
after he'd revealed himself as the Son of God?
He lived here, where you dwell,
talking about the laws of nature,
but I prefer to call it about "Death".

Now, Rheginos, the Son of God,
was also the Son of Man, he included both
through his essential humanity and divinity,
so in one way he could conquer death
by being God's chosen Son, and also as Son of Man
he could bring about the restoration of the pleroma.

He came from heaven as a seed of truth
before the universe was created;
in this form many powers and deities came into being.

I know I'm giving you the "Answer"
in somewhat complex terminology,
but in reality there's nothing complicated
in the Word of Truth.

The "Answer" appeared
so as not to leave any point as secretive,
and to show everything openly

regarding Existence, the end of wickedness,
and the revelation handed to those Chosen.

This "Answer" is an emergence of Truth and Spirit,
from which Grace flows abundantly;
Christ devoured Death, as you know,
for he renounced the decaying world
and transmuted himself into an eternal Aeon.

And he lifted himself up,
having devoured the seen by the unseen,
and demonstrated the path of Eternal Life;
then, as Paul said, "we suffered, rose up,
and went to heaven with him".

Now if we're in this life, clad in his robes,
we also dispense his light,
and we're received by him until our physical death.

We're attracted heavenwards by him like rays from the Sun,
not being held back by any power;
this is the spiritual resurrection,
which devours the mental and the bodily function.

If there are those who can't believe
they are probably unfit to be convinced;
for, my son, it's the Kingdom of Faith,

and not that which belongs to argument.

If there's one who believes
among the world's pedagogues
that the dead will rise up,
then that scholar will also ascend.

But don't let the philosopher think that he who returns
by himself to himself is to be trusted,
as it's a matter of Faith, rather than reason.

For we've known, seen, and met the Son of Man
and we have faith that he rose up from the dead.

This is Christ of whom we sing
"he was the slayer of death, he's great,
and in him we trust,
strong are those who have perfect Faith".

The thoughts and minds of those who are saved
shall never die!
So we're chosen for salvation and redemption,
as we're preordained from birth
not to trip into the deep pit of folly,
preached by charlatans without experience.

We'll come into the divine wisdom

of those who've known Truth;
Truth which is safeguarded can never be renounced!

Strong is the formation of the Pleroma;
small is that fragment which broke away
and became this world.

"The Whole" is what's embraced,
it hasn't emerged into being,
it was primordially pre-existing.

So Rheginos, never doubt the resurrection,
for if you weren't pre-existing in a body
before you were born,
you acquired one when you came into life.

So why won't you acquire a form
when you rise up into the Aeon?
That which is superior to a mortal body
is that Spirit which is the cause of life.

Surely that Self which came into Being as your own
is yours, and lives with you,
yet while you endure this world what is your greatest need?
This is what you have been making
earnest effort to understand!

The aftermath of the body is senility
yet is your Real Self impure?
You can count upon lack of a body as a great gain,
for you won't lose what is superior,
the Spirit, when you depart.

That flesh which is inferior is diminished,
but even then grace supervenes,
nothing saves us from the world
but the "Whole" that we are, that's our salvation!
We've been given salvation from beginning to end,
let's contemplate this way.

Some earnestly wish to comprehend
in the self-enquiry which they pursue,
whether he'll be saved immediately
when he leaves the body?

Beyond doubt, only the spiritually alive will be saved,
not the unspiritual dead!
What then does the Resurrection mean?
It is the revelation of those who've arisen.

The Bible tells us that Elijah and Moses
reappeared after death,
it wasn't a delusion but real;
in fact the world is a delusion

rather than the Resurrection,
which is in Being through our Lord
and Saviour, Jesus Christ!

But what I'm telling you now is important;
those apparently living unspiritually shall perish;
the wealthy will rot in poverty,
the kings will be cast down,
all is subject to change, the world is delusion,
I must refrain, or I'll complain to excess!

But the Resurrection isn't transient,
it's established truth,
it's the revelation of "what really is",
transmutation, transmigration
and metempsychosis, into new life.

The undying descends on the dying,
light dissolves the darkness,
the pleroma supplies any lack;
these are the emblems of resurrection,
Christ makes it benevolent.

So don't think partially Rheginos,
nor dwell in harmony with the flesh,
because others do;
but flee from separation and its chains,

and you'll enjoy resurrection now!

For if he who is certain of his death,
even if he's old, is brought to this state,
why not believe yourself to be risen now,
and live as resurrected?

If you feel resurrected, but go on
as if you are to die as a mortal,
why should I ignore your lack of spiritual exercise.
It's right for each to practise in different ways
to be released from the fear of death
so he won't fall into delusion,
but shall again be what he originally was.

This knowledge I have accepted from the benevolence
and grace of our Lord Jesus Christ;
I've taught you and my brothers,
not leaving out anything,
which will reinforce your faith.

If there is anything stated that's unclear
in my explanation of the Word,
I'll try to make it clearer for you,
whenever you enquire.

So don't be envious of anybody in your brotherhood
if he can help; many are investigating what I've told you;
to all those, I pray peace and grace shall be with them;
I welcome you and all who love you in brotherly love!

THE VISION OF GOD

A fragment from Valentinus, circa AD 150. An Egyptian steeped in Hellenistic culture, active in Alexandria, influenced by Basilides, Philo, and Gnostic Christianity. He stresses the necessity for a vision of the Divine.

One there IS who's perfect and good;
His way of speaking to us is through the gift of His son.

Through him only can a soul become flawless
when all wickedness has been expelled from the heart.

The many ghosts dwelling in the heart
don't allow it to become pure, instead,
each carries out its own deeds obliviously and ignorantly,
defiling the soul in different ways with desire and self-will.

The heart suffers as in a caravan procession,
the sandy desert is full of pit holes,
dug by humans and filled with their shit.

While they're there the caravan party live in a vile way
and behave disregarding the rights of the place

where they temporarily live.

The heart too is defiled by being the home of demonic desires
until it sees the primal light, prior to all light.

But when the Father visits the heart He purifies her
and fills her with radiance making her sanctified.

Such a man or woman is truly blest
for that soul will know God.

Further Reading

The Gnostic Religion, Hans Jonas, Beacon Press 1958

Hermetica, Brian Copenhauer, Cambridge U.P. 1992

The Nag Hammadi Library, Ed. James M Robinson, E J Brill 1987

The Gnostic Scriptures, Bentley Layton, Doubleday 1987

The Gnostic Gospels, Elaine Pagels, Random House 1979